"*The Power of How* is the most meaningful book I have read regarding authentic leadership. This book is easy to read and provides excellent "Take Actions" sections at the end of every Chapter. Courageous leadership is needed today more than ever. It takes mental, emotional and physical grit. A true inside out job. This life changing journey will not only positively impact your life, but more importantly, those you have the privilege to lead."
- Christina Gullo, President and CEO of Villa of Hope

"Wow, just read *The Power of* How. What a powerful guide for all of us on the leadership journey. This really helped me ground myself again. Every leader should read this book."
- Angelica Perez-Delgado, President and CEO of Ibero-American Action League

"*The Power of How* is chock full of practices that I can immediately implement. I felt as though the book was written just for me and the challenges I face as a business owner! I have been starting each day with a chapter from the book and visualizing how I can put the concept into use that day. There hasn't been a day the topic hasn't been helpful."
- Peter Messner, President of Messner Flooring

"*The Power of How*" mirrors the gift of Mary and Ed's work with individuals and organizations. This book serves as a solid, researched guide that any of us can refer to. It puts courageous leadership into best practices and actions in both our professional and personal lives. It is a book that I will continue to use as a "go-to" guide on my leadership journey."
- Kim Brumber, President and CEO of East House

"*The Power of How* has had a profound impact on me in both my professional and personal life. It provides simple processes and language that actively drives continuous learning. I now have the definitive manual for developing myself as a servant leader for the betterment of my employees, company and our community."
- Eric Wangler, President and CEO of Jaccard Corporation

THE POWER OF HOW™

Transform Fear and Self-Doubt

into Leading and Living with Courage

Mary L. Burkhardt and Edward E. Davison-Gwynn

Copyright Page

LeadPeakPerformance.com

585-362-9196 | 585-414-2002

mary@leadpeakperformance.com

ed@leadpeakperformance.com

We dedicate this book to all the Courageous Leaders we have had the privilege to work with, gotten to know, and traveled alongside on their Courageous Leadership journey.

Table of Contents

Preface

We created *The Power of How™: Transform Fear and Self-Doubt into Leading and Living with Courage* to explore the most frequent and relevant questions and interests of our clients. Our book is a quick reference to dive into the most essential personal and professional leadership challenges and opportunities.

The Power of How™ is organized into our top-10 leadership capabilities with three '*how*' discussions in each chapter. This book is a valuable guide as similar challenges and opportunities present themselves on your leadership journey and throughout your life.

We are *Leaders Working with Leaders™* discussing questions from leaders on how to be increasingly successful. Leadership growth is all about becoming a freer and more courageous person.

We designed and wrote this book to be a key resource for you on your courageous leadership and life journey. It is truly your wildest adventure ever!

Introduction

When leadership is distilled to its core, we are left with two words. These two words describe how leaders can maintain a positive attitude and create the inspiring, motivating environment people desire. They are the foundation of high-performing individuals, teams and organizations. These two words are *ENERGY and INFLUENCE*. What *energy* do I choose to bring to any situation and how does that *energy* first *influence* me and then those around me? These are the fundamental personal and professional questions that will guide the concepts throughout this book. We cannot give away what we don't have.

This growth and transformation is life-changing as we continually overcome fear and self-doubt and live into our true powerful selves. Resilience, grit and indomitable spirit are themes you will find throughout this book. We believe the powerful journey of leadership is not for the faint of heart.

Having awareness first of self, with all our self-talk, fears, intentions and beliefs, and then of others is a leader's way of consistently monitoring whether or not (s)he is bringing positive energy to their environment. Research shows that we each have about 60,000 thoughts or 6,000 thought-units in a day.[2,3,4] This constant narrative running in our minds generates feelings throughout our day that we may or may not be conscious of. It is so easy to get swept away in our stream of thoughts and feelings. We tell ourselves a story, and then we believe it.

If you were to ask just about any leader how they are feeling, most will tell you they are tired, stressed and anxious about something.

We are programmed to focus on the negative feelings, thoughts and emotions more than the positive. About 80%[5,6,7,8] of our thoughts are negative or concerning. We are biologically wired for immediate survival and therefore fearful of any threat. We are not wired for long-term positivity and enthusiasm.

Developing ourselves to have more positive self-talk not only helps us be more effective leaders in our personal and professional lives, it is critical for our health and well-being. The medical profession shares this adds an average of ten years to our lifespan.[1]

We often ask leaders we work with to share their *essence.* This reflection is where leadership truly begins. We are not asking for thoughts and feelings (we all have plenty of worries, fears, self-doubts and second-guessing). We are asking them how they are choosing to be. We begin by leading ourselves, and we are all leaders of our lives. We ask leaders to decide their *essence*:

> *"In spite of all the circumstances we are facing at any given time, what energy am I choosing to bring to my life and work in this moment – the best energy I can bring for myself and to best*

impact others in our work and time together right now?"

With this question, we are intentionally moving past thoughts and feelings to *being* our best selves to all our relationships and life's work. Circumstances have always been around, and they will still be here long after we are gone.

Our personal and professional leadership challenge is to choose who and how we want to be in spite of these conditions. Thus, we willfully relax and release our *energy* from being caught up in this ever-changing world. This awareness is where each of our life moments bring us to strength and resolve or are lost to the control of external factors.

We begin with leading ourselves; therefore, we are all leaders, regardless of titles. How we choose to lead ourselves will determine how we *influence* those around us at home and at work. Some of the best leaders we've met in our lives had no formal title. They chose to bring *energy* that inspired themselves and others.

To get to *essence*, some questions leaders can ask themselves are the following:

- Am I in control of my thoughts and feelings, or am I reflecting what I'm experiencing around me?

- Am I choosing my *essence,* or is my *energy* being determined by circumstances out of my control so that I let myself become a victim?

- Am I bringing my best self in service of the **purpose** of the work we want to accomplish or am I distracted by negative thoughts and feelings?

Most of us have experienced managers who people constantly wondered…

- *"What mood is the boss in today?"*

- *"Do you think this is a good day to give the boss this news, or should I just wait until tomorrow?"*

Their lack of predictability does not foster trusting relationships and productive cultures.

If we don't understand the impact we are having on ourselves and others based on intentionally choosing what **energy** we are bringing, the amount of **influence** we have diminishes. Fear and self-doubt are extremely contagious. The good news is, so is positivity and claiming our power!

When we break down years of employee polls and surveys on leadership, hundreds of surveys we've administered and collected ourselves, and our combined 100+ years of experience *asking* team members we've led, the two most important factors for high-performing people, teams and organizations are the following:

1. Having a direct leader with a positive attitude.

2. Feeling like the environment created by leadership is motivating and inspiring.

When we think about *energy and influence* as being the two key aspects and definition of what leadership is, the question becomes, how do I bring my best *energy* to myself and to *influence* those around me?

We often hear in conversations with leaders about things that are not within their control. When our *energy* is focused on things out of our control (for example, the economy, political environment, the weather, anything we can't directly *influence*) that "thing" gets bigger and bigger, and we diminish our *influence* on what is within our control. We have a finite amount of *energy* and our brains are tremendous at conserving that *energy*. When we focus our *energy* on what's within our control, that "thing" gets bigger and bigger, and we can expand our *influence*, creating worthy, productive futures and healthy lives.

Take Action:

Some things leaders can do to expand their *influence* versus diminishing it:

1. Having a clear understanding of what is within and what is out of their control. Ignoring threats and outside conditions is not what we are suggesting. We need awareness of what is out there and then focus our best self to make a positive difference.

2. Asking, *"What are the things I can focus on to make the situation better?"* even if it's small things.

3. Asking, *"How do I need to be to expand my **influence**?"*

As a leader, *and we all are leaders*, awareness and leveraging of our **energy** and expanding our **influence** is a life-long process. Awareness of and transcending our fears and self-doubt is the path to being who we were born to be, to live our powerful best selves.

Essence and **mindfulness** are absolute *life-changers* to forever live your best energetic life.

Who would want to live their brief life experience any other way?

Join us now for your wildest transformational journey through *The Power of How: Transform Fear and Self-Doubt Into Leading and Living with Courage.*

The Power of How™
Transform Fear and Self-Doubt Into
Leading and Living with Courage
Model

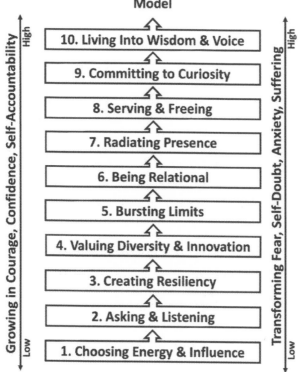

Growing in Courage, Confidence, Self-Accountability — High / Low

Transforming Fear, Self-Doubt, Anxiety, Suffering — High / Low

10. Living Into Wisdom & Voice
9. Committing to Curiosity
8. Serving & Freeing
7. Radiating Presence
6. Being Relational
5. Bursting Limits
4. Valuing Diversity & Innovation
3. Creating Resiliency
2. Asking & Listening
1. Choosing Energy & Influence

Chapter 1

Courageous Leadership Is
Relational Energy and Influence

*Deeply notice and give meaning to reality to "what
things really are."*

How Courageous Leaders Choose Their Essence to Find Their Best Energy for Leading

When we work with teams, we start every session with each person sharing a word to describe their best *essence* for our time together. Beginning with a word of *essence* seems like such a simple thing, but it is actually one of the hardest things to do. How do *Courageous Leaders* choose their *essence* to find their best *energy*?

Each time we meet, we begin our work with teams by asking each person to share, *"What essence are you choosing to bring for our time together today?"*

We don't begin by asking how people are feeling or what they are thinking, resulting in a flood of thoughts and feelings. Instead, we ask people how they are *choosing to be*.

If we ask most adults we talk with how they are doing, most will tell us they feel tired, stressed, anxious or concerned about something.

The question is, in spite of what we're feeling and thinking, can we choose one word to describe our *essence* that is in the best service to ourselves and those we are with in our time together? In any moment, wherever we find ourselves—at home, work, socially— what *essence* can we choose to bring forward?

The running narrative we have in our mind is constant. Since we have about 60,000 thoughts a day,[2,3,4] often we aren't even aware of how many of our thoughts are generating fear and self-doubt. When we choose our *essence,* we become the watcher of our thoughts and feelings. We understand that we are generating our thoughts and feelings. It is up to us to *choose* how we want to be.

Many people initially struggle with this question because they don't want to feel like they're being fake or like they're not acknowledging a very real circumstance. We don't suggest that people ignore their thoughts or repress their feelings. There will always be circumstances and a streaming narrative in our minds about what those circumstances mean.

Regardless of the circumstances, what is the best *energy* we can bring to any moment of time by choosing our *essence*?

Essence is *energy.* While we're having these 60,000 thoughts a day and thousands of feelings, ask, *"Who and how do I want to be right now?"* When we decide how we want and need to be, we can bring our best *energy* forward and be that *essence.*

We still have all kinds of thoughts and feelings. A client of ours once called it *summoning. "What am I going to summon for myself to take me forward?"*

So, it's not thoughts or feelings that we are after. We're acknowledging the thoughts and feelings that we have every second, and then we are asking, *"What is the one word of* **essence** *that we choose to bring forward?"*

3

Each moment of life is a choice to be our best selves while positively impacting ourselves and others.

Essence helps in many ways, including the following:

- Helping us to be emotionally regulated in spite of circumstances, as they will be constantly changing.

- Giving us the energy and the stability for how we want and need to be in our work, at home and anywhere we find ourselves on life's journey.

- Helping us be our best selves and not be controlled by the random thoughts and feelings we have in a day. This is letting go of the "chattering mind" in order to find clarity, tame fear and relax into releasing useless negative worry-anxiety energy.

While the thoughts and feelings we have may be legitimate, they can be very distracting and draining to the energy we need to have for a particular situation. We ask,

> *"Who do I need to be now, and what energy do I need to bring to this moment, in the best service for myself and others?"*

When leadership is distilled to its core, we are left with two words that describe how we can maintain an uplifting attitude and create the inspiring, motivating environment that is healthy for us, desired by our

4

families at home and by our work teams. These two words are:

ENERGY and INFLUENCE.

> **What *energy* do I choose to bring to any situation, and how does that *energy influence* first me and then those around me?**

We can't give away something we don't have or have not first created for ourselves.

Having awareness first of self and then of others is the way to consistently monitor whether or not disciplined positive energy is thriving in the environment.

How Courageous Leaders Up Their Self-Awareness and Their Awareness of Others

Our approach to life is going to determine how life responds to us. If we give good *energy* to what is in our control and what we can *influence*, then we're going to see the results of that reflected back to us through life, through others, and through the results we create. How do *Courageous Leaders* up their self-awareness and their awareness of others?

When we expend energy and focus on things out of our control, we don't have the energy it takes to focus on the things that are within our control.

It's a yes-or-no life. We can accomplish something, or we can focus on things that are not in our control, saying, *"Well I tried, I tried, I tried."*

In the long run, we either did something, or we didn't do it. It has everything to do with our mindset.

The world is a mirror that generally reflects back exactly what we put out. To change our results, we must change our energy, and to change our energy, we must change our thoughts. With everything we know, what is the best way to take charge of our life and to accomplish our *goals*?

There is a simple quote from author Peter Senge that captures the essence of this idea, *"Every time we think the problem is out there, that very thought is the problem."*

Given the circumstances, given everything that's out of my control, what can I do? What is the next best thing I can do to keep moving forward?

We often speak with our clients about the power of self-talk and how developing self-talk can prevent them from being hijacked by negative thought loops.

We ask clients, *"Who do you talk to most?"* and the answer is usually their spouse or their children. We wait and ask again, *"Who do you really talk to the most?"* It's fun to see the light bulb go on when they realize, *"I actually talk to myself the most, more than I talk to anyone else."*

The data about our conscious awake time is very humbling. It shows that we spend about 80%[5,6,7,8] of our awake time saying negative things to ourselves about life, work, others and the world. When we think this way, gravity pulls down, and we pull ourselves down with negative self-talk. We are not only disempowering ourselves but also creating a very stressful self.

We have been doing our own studies for a number of years. For example, when we get on an elevator, it is a perfect lab. We'll say, *"Oh, this is just a lovely day."* It may be raining or snowing, but it is a lovely day, as we are fortunate to have this day on earth. Very often, we'll get back the response, for instance, if it is a sunny day, *"We will most certainly pay for this nice day later in the week!"* Or if it's been a nice summer, the response will be, *"Just wait, we will really pay for this in the winter!"*

If it's snowing, the responses are often even more negative. We actually have to think these things before we say them out loud. For years, we've run this impromptu personal study. We would say something positive, and very, very few times, we would get back, *"Yes, this is a lovely day,"* and leave it right there.

We believe that life truly is a timed activity. So, the question is, how intentional are we? Are we on remote control and sort of mechanical?

Are we actually taking control of our life, or is everything else in control, such as the weather, other people or circumstances?

If we are not in control, then who is in control? We give away our power so everyone and everything else is in control.

If we're saying things like, *"We are going to pay for this,"* and so forth, the issue really is that we are having those thoughts first. We have a lot of thoughts in a day, and if 80% of them are negative self-talk, what are we doing to ourselves? We observe and read about people being stressed out and burned out. Is it really everything else stressing us out, or are we unknowingly stressing our own selves out with our unaware thinking and behaviors?

Life is a self-fulfilling prophecy. It is the outcome of our thinking and our actions. It's going to be exactly what we make of it—no more and no less.

Leaders tell us they are distracted by many things. They come to work in the morning feeling focused and energetic, but a lot comes up during the day, and they feel they haven't accomplished what they had planned.

Take Action:

Here are three things we believe are important for a strong inner voice:

1. **Be very clear about the *vision* to *strategically*** position the organization for the future. When leaders look at themselves in the mirror, they ask themselves, *"What is my vision as a leader?"* Seeing the *vision* and all the outcomes that enable a *vision* gives leaders wonderful direction regardless of what they are dealing with.

2. **Be very clear about the *mission*.** Leaders take time to ask themselves, *"What is my personal mission?"* Are they doing the work of their personal *mission*? Are they doing something they just can't live without doing? Something they are born to do, have talent to do, and a burning desire inside to do? That's actually a personal *mission*.

3. **Be very clear on their *personal values*.** This means, *"What would I really take a stand for based on my values?"* and, *"If this comes up, what would I do?"*

We believe that if your inner voice is well-grounded...

1. Its foundation is a reflection of who you want to be as a leader.

2. It is aligned with your *purpose* on earth—what you were born to contribute to this life.

3. It is crystal clear on your *values*, which will make everything else easy. You will always be able to answer these questions:

   o What can I do now?

   o What will I do next?

   o Will I be trusted to do the best next right thing versus what is easy, self-serving or fast?

We think this practice is really the heart of the leader and the heart of the inner-voice. If those answers are clear, it is likely that leaders will have the emotional regulation, discipline and determination to prioritize their day's work and most important outcomes. In fact, they will face, understand and grow from their self-doubts and fears, being the *Courageous Leader* to those they lead and impact.

Developing our ability to choose our *essence* in any moment takes a high level of self-awareness and other-awareness.

Take Action

When we think about *energy and influence* as the definition of leadership, some questions for leaders arise:

- How do I become more aware of and determine what *energy* I bring to any situation?

- Am I aware of how my *energy influences* those around me?

- Does my *energy* inspire people to bring their best, or does my *energy* create fear, anxiety or stress?

- How can I have better awareness and control over my *energy* moment to moment?

Who we are and what we do has a much larger impact on our *influence* than our title or position.

The Ancient Greeks spoke of three spheres that determine to a great degree the amount of *influence* a person has.

🔥 *Ethos* – The ethics or character of the leader. Can people always count on me and trust me to do what I say I will do? Am I true to my *values*?

11

 ✷ **Pathos** – Appeal to people on an emotional level. Do they care deeply about the *purpose* of their work? Do I speak to this passion?

 ✷ **Logos** – Appeal to people on a logical/rational level. Do they understand and participate in the rationale behind decision-making regarding their work? Do I speak to this logic and honor their thinking and perspectives?

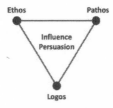

Take Action

Additional questions for leaders:

- To expand my *influence*, do I need to focus more *energy* on a desired outcome?

- Am I having a thought that encourages me and others to go to action or a thought that gives us an excuse not to have the courage to act?

- Am I filled with fear and self-doubt that causes hesitation, or am I *excuse-free* and *self-accountable*? How many of us evolve to be excuse-free, meaning being congruent with what we say and what we do?

We don't believe that positional authority has anything to do with leadership. Getting someone to do something because we have a position of power over them gets, at best, compliance. Managing through compliance may get things done temporarily while the manager is there commanding and demanding. When the manager isn't around, people will not be inspired to give their best. This is very different than inspiring and igniting engagement through *energy and influence*.

How Courageous Leaders Use Awareness of Others to Influence Their Leadership

It has been said that people quit bad managers, not bad companies. We hear stories so very often that support this statement. Many divorces and failed relationships are also the result of a lack of awareness of partners and family members. How do *Courageous Leaders* use awareness of others to help *influence* their leadership?

The *influence* leaders have, both positive and negative, cannot be overstated. If leaders are consumed by fear and self-doubt, the teams they lead will be unstable and reflect that fear.

With awareness of others, leaders can use positive energy to create and sustain motivating, inspiring environments. Without this awareness, leaders miss subtle (or not so subtle) cues that things aren't well.

Characteristics of positive environments created by leaders include:

- A shared *mission* that is bigger than themselves and one in which they can see themselves.

- The ability for team members to make personal progress through their development and new opportunities for them to help advance.

- Trusting relationships within the organization that provide a sense of community and facilitate easier communications and coordination to get things done.

🔥 Team members have enough autonomy to make decisions and take reasonable risks that are right for the business without worrying about unnecessary red tape or fear.

Positive leaders who consistently create positive work environments not only help their teams deliver the best results, but they also enable people on their teams and in their organizations to live more meaningful and positive lives.

People who go home at the end of the day from positive work environments tend to have a more positive home life with their families. Kids grow up in happier, more positive homes. Partners talk to each other more in friendly, constructive conversations.

Things others would label as problems and complications, to a person in this state of flow, are challenges to overcome and part of the journey to the next peak. Life is an exciting adventure to people in flow, and the internal flames of those around them are *ignited* too.

Take Action

Questions for leaders to ask themselves:

1. Do you think team members go home and talk more with their family as a result of a positive workday experience?

2. Do team members view what are usually considered "mistakes" as learning opportunities?

3. Do you expect and require a certain number of "waves" and failure, reflecting that team members are taking risks to learn, grow and advance their organization?

4. Do you believe pain is a valuable part of life and growth and therefore worth it to evolve and grow?

When we lead ourselves, our teams and our organizations to ever-better Peak Performance, we are in a state of growth and our internal flame is *ignited*. We can see it in people's eyes when they're in this state of flow.

Their eyes shine when they discuss their life and their work. They do not come from fear, but from love for their work and life.

Ultimately, they are curious about what each of their fears and doubts can teach them about themselves. What thoughts, energies and actions need to be transcended beyond fear and self-doubt to more life-giving thoughts, emotions and actions?

STEAR Model™

S	T	E	A	R
i	h	m	c	e
t	o	o	t	s
u	u	t	i	u
a	g	i	o	l
t	h	o	n	t
i	t	n		
o	s	s		
n				

Mindset: Understanding our fears and negative thoughts is part of our life path to revisit what we are thinking to create a more life-giving, helpful thought, which generates a more self-empowered action and desired results.

The fact that the majority of thoughts are negative or concerning can be helpful in many situations. The reason we have this default negative mode is biology and survival.

We've survived as a species by thinking negatively about potential threats. For example, we may not have a positive feeling about something unknown rustling in a bush. My decision to avoid the bush based on that negative feeling can be very positive if there is a saber-toothed tiger hiding in the bush. I may not have even noticed the rustling if my feeling of danger hadn't alerted me to the movement and noise in the bush. The feeling (and my decision to understand it and make a positive action based on it) saved my life.

In our modern lives, feelings can sometimes take over, and it can be difficult to take the time and effort to backtrack and determine where they're actually coming from. This can cause us to lose objectivity and eventually control of our emotions and rational brain. It is so easy for us to over-dramatize and spook ourselves.

Leaders who understand how to use this essential tool (feelings)—critical for our very survival—as an **alert system** can have a tremendous advantage. Recognizing (in self and others) that feelings are not a weakness is the first step. The more intense the feeling, the bigger the need may be to understand it and what it is alerting us to.

Take Action:

To better pay attention to and use feelings as an alert-system, we can increase self-awareness as well as coach others to do the same by doing the following:

1. When we experience a feeling that has a negative effect on our own life or our interactions with someone else, try to determine first what the feeling is. Stop and ask, *"What feeling(s) am I having in this moment?"*

2. Next ask, *"What is this feeling trying to alert me to?"* Often this awareness alone can be helpful.

3. Next, *"How am I at risk?"* Never move so fast as to underestimate the power of risks.

4. Ask, *"How will I mitigate risks?"*

5. The next question is (if action is needed), *"What next right action can I take based on these insights?"*

As simple as they may sound, taking the time to work through these five steps can lead to the discovery of new intuitive and creative paths through long standing fears and self-doubts that have created barriers in our lives.

Understanding what an advantage it is to use feelings as an alert system can help us be more aware of our own selves as well as being more productive in building relationships and enhanced communication with others.

19

Chapter 2

Courageous Leaders Don't Tell What They Can Ask

Stay in your leadership lane to avoid doing for others what they can do for themselves.

How Courageous Leaders Tame Their Reactive Brains by Slowing Down to Understand People

One of the key jobs of a leader is to coach those they lead to develop critical-thinking skills and to solve whatever challenges they face. Often, we're so busy that when someone comes and asks us a question, the immediate reaction is to give them an answer or to problem-solve for them. How do *Courageous Leaders* tame their reactive brains by slowing down to understand people?

> *Leadership is a constant battle against expediency.*

The expedient action in conversation is to give immediate answers—to tell versus to ask. If someone says something that doesn't sit right, the tendency is to react versus finding out their intentions. In hindsight, leaders often wish they could put words back in their own mouths. As the saying goes, it's hard to put toothpaste back in the tube!

Leadership means we are being intentional about *pausing* and *responding* instead of reacting. This gives us a chance to check out our thoughts before we put them into the world. When we take a moment to pause, we may see things differently. When we react immediately, we often fail to truly understand where the other person is coming from and what self-doubt and fears they hold.

Leaders often tell us that, in the whirlwind of the day, there's not time to *stop and ask* so they give solutions. We see it as *pay me now or pay me later.* Putting in a little more effort to get people to come up with the solution may take more time up front but it's going to pay dividends in the long-term when people can think for themselves.

Leaders are constantly building dependence or independence in others.

Stopping and asking an internal question helps leaders develop their inner-coach.

Take Action

If we feel a reaction to something internally, intentionally ***stop and ask*** the following:

- *"Why am I feeling this way?"*

- *"What's causing me to feel this way?"*

- *"Am I fearing a loss of control or not being right?"*

Pausing and asking these internal questions gives us a chance to choose our response instead of reacting.

Calming and controlling our reactive mind is a fulltime job.

It has been said that humans are creatures of emotion, not reason. Leaders working with people will inevitably be triggered from time to time. In conversations with team members, leaders may suddenly realize they feel offended and defensive about what was said. They may react too quickly to a question and regret what they said.

By asking that question, we come from a place of understanding. Thus, the much talked about and written about *critical thinking skills* will actually be used when those we lead practice doing the work for themselves.

When leaders (with the best intentions) do *for others* instead of teaching and coaching, they create "learned-helplessness" in those they lead. This is a most contagious, life-robbing condition caught from leaders who don't go first with trusting others to learn, grow and perform and is usually based in fear and self-doubt.

The question leaders need to ask is, *"Am I fearful of not being as important and needed, and what work will I do next if others don't need me?"*

When leaders step into a role leading a new team, often they're trying to learn both the work and also how the team operates. The team may do things in a different way than the new leader would do them.

Take Action

Courageous Leaders start off on the right foot with new teams without creating fear and self-doubt by asking the following questions:

1. **What is our *purpose (mission)*?**

   By beginning with "listening and learning tours," new leaders can discuss guiding *values* and establish common *goals*.

   The way to integrate ideas into a new team is to begin by talking about *purpose*, common *goals*, common *beliefs* and important ways of being (*values*).

   Once common *goals* are established, leaders work to help each team member understand how their individual *goals* are aligned to the common *goals*. Changes are now related to something personal for each team member.

   This approach is very different from any of the following conclusions:

   - *"Things are just different now."*

   - *"We need to do things differently here."*

   - *"That's just the way it is."*

   It's very hard for people to fall in love with new ideas and new ways of doing the work using that approach.

2. How can I involve the team in decision-making?

Once the team has agreed on a path forward and has mutual understanding of the importance of the work to be done, it's critically important to have team members involved in the decision-making process as much as possible.

Having choices, being able to see the contributions they're making, getting feedback on the contributions they're making, and being appreciated for the contributions they're making are all important for team members to truly feel involved and valued.

People, within a structure, need to have choices and have some say in how they do their work with feedback on how their contribution is helping the team be productive in the move forward.

Having input and being heard is the path to involvement and engagement for each person.

3. What are positive actions and behaviors, and how will they be recognized and rewarded?

Leaders find ways to reward people for what they do well versus criticizing them for what they do wrong. Some of the easiest and most meaningful ways to consistently reward positive behaviors and actions is by noticing, complementing, and saying, *"Thank you."*

There are many ways to recognize and reward people. Actually knowing each team member's strengths and contributions helps the leader give specific feedback that is meaningful to each person individually. Each person needs to know they are doing important work and that the organization is better as a result of their talent, energy and good work.

A sincere compliment or reinforcement and being recognized for the contributions they are making are all important for team members to feel involved and valued. That's really part of the science of human behavior and how people tick!

4. **Am I consistently being appropriately vulnerable and real?**

When leaders are appropriately vulnerable and real, it enables others to be open and honest about what's going well and where they're having struggles. The leader doesn't appear to be too perfect, holding back from what *they* could improve or do better.

> **When we are approachable and real, others can be open and honest about what's going well and where they're having struggles.**

If the leader appears too buttoned-up, they don't get the real truth from those they're leading. When leaders go first, pointing out what they could do better, those they lead can be more real about what is going well and not so well with their work. Constant improvement is an okay and comfortable discussion. Fear and self-doubt are stamped out.

When leading a new team or implementing any changes and improvements, these four questions are critical in helping team members say, *"I love working with our leader,"* and, *"I love the work we do as a team."*

When team members have common **goals**, choices and input into decisions, they feel really good about their contributions because they are noticed, recognized and rewarded, and feel open and comfortable with the leader. Who wouldn't want to work with a leader like this?

As leaders advance in organizations, they often find themselves leading areas where they do not have expertise. When one finds themselves in such situations, it can be an incredible leadership opportunity. The first ninety days leading in a new area are critical.

A few common mistakes leaders make when leading a new team include the following:

- Failing to do an initial "listening tour" to really learn about their new organization and its team members.

- Trying to gain respect by saying things such as, *"I am here, I am in charge and this is the way it will be now."*

- Attempting to impose solutions that worked in a previous role without truly understanding current issues.

- Talking a lot in meetings early on. Leaders often consciously or unconsciously feel the need to prove they deserve the job. The result is often the opposite.

- Bragging or talking about previous successes. Moving forward by looking in the rearview mirror seldom works.

- Not interacting with the new team members enough. Servant leaders who are focused on making their teams look good ahead of themselves are far more effective.

Take Action

When leading a new team:

- Find out what success looks like from the start. Ask the person you report to what success would look like.

- Talk with the person you report to about **goals** and the **timeframes** for achieving them, and how you and the team will be measured. Be very specific and clear in your understanding. Never rush past documenting this understanding for regular review with whomever you report to.

- Find ways to get acquainted with background for the new group, including markets, challenges and an introduction to the technologies involved.

- Clarify **strategy** and connect with your team. The real work starts when you establish what success looks like with your new team, when you form new relationships and when you identify **values** (and behaviors) by which you will work together.

- Create shared **mission** and **vision statements** for the future with your team so it is theirs from the start. Translate the overall **goals** into a **winning strategy** with the team and be clear on each person's role and self-accountability.

- Feel the pulse of the business. Set up regular one-on-ones with your direct reports and weekly team member work-sessions. It's the best and fastest way to get to know each other and to establish how you want to lead with them.

- Learn where you need to focus. This kind of engagement also quickly gives you a heads-up on the areas that need your attention. You can notice what is and is not working and, with the team, bring forward the needed areas for improvement.

When the leader is disciplined, determined and persistent in daily learning, and when they value the contributions of others, the very best is brought forth from the team to achieve its shared *goals*.

The Japanese proverb, *"Fall down seven times, get up eight,"* is pure gold for developing the resilience to continuously lead teams, organizations and communities to outstanding performance.

With this mindset, failure to achieve expectations is not an option.

When leaders engage and empower their teams, it reinforces the value they place in the team's expertise and their ability to perform. Asking questions while learning and noticing the contribution of each team member builds trust and strong relationships. With humility and the will to keep moving forward, leaders can continue their journey from Peak to Peak, even in areas where they are not the technical expert.

What leaders do to earn their way to lead will change many times in their career, but *how* they learn to lead will be the real constant value they add, regardless of where they are leading. When we look at the secret sauce of the leader, this is it. Any business or operation is just an intricate web of relationships.

When we ask all successful leaders to what they owe their success, they say, *"Creating and sustaining positive, trusting relationships."*

How Courageous Leaders Tame the Reactive Brain

Choosing to respond versus reacting to a stimulus can put us in two completely different universes. The time we take between stimulus and response makes all the difference. How do *Courageous Leaders* tame the reactive brain?

The most powerful quote we've heard on choosing to respond versus reacting to any situation is from Holocaust survivor, psychiatrist and author, Viktor Frankl. Frankl said in his book, *Man's Search for Meaning*:

> ***"Between stimulus and response there is a space. In that space is our power to choose our response. In our response lies our growth and our freedom."***

If we use our time to be intentional and constructive in our response instead of reactionary it makes all the difference in the world.

Take Action

33

Here are some ways the best leaders we've worked with condition themselves to pause and give themselves time before reacting to any situation.

Some of the most tried and true ideas are:

1. **Stop and ask**:

   Before responding, remember to stop (some people literally picture a stop sign in their minds) and ask an internal question. The question may be, *"What is the best question I can ask right now?"* The action of pausing in the moment and asking ourselves a question is more important than the question we ask.

2. *Essence* **and** *essence-symbol*:

   When we work with groups of leaders on development, we ask them to identify an *essence-symbol or image*. When leaders practice using their *essence-symbol or image*, they can see it in their mind's eye, and at any time, they can bring themselves to the present moment. By seeing an *essence-symbol or image*, leaders can choose their best **essence**. *Essence-symbols* help to center, calm and slow ourselves down, allowing us to choose our response in any situation.

3. **The Three Buddhist Gates:**

   The Buddhist practice of screening thoughts through three "gates" before speaking helps many leaders we've worked with. The three gates are:

- Is what I am about to say truthful? *(Am I sure?)*

- Is what I'm about to say kind? *(Is it helpful?)*

- Is what I am about to say necessary? *(If so, am I the best person to say it?)*

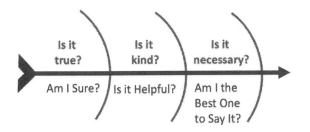

These three questions allow us time to choose our response wisely rather than just reacting.

4. **Countdown** (The 10-second rule):

   A simple practice is counting down from 10 before responding to important questions. This practice is not only simple, it is also backed by science. Our emotional brain fires almost immediately when triggered. The rational (executive) part of our brain takes about 4-8 seconds to fire.[9] There is great wisdom in the advice we were given as children to count down from 10 when we are upset!

5. **What, So What, Now What?** Another way to give the rational mind time to catch up to our

emotional mind is to ask the *what, now what, so what* questions about the situation.

- What? – What exactly is the situation?

- So What? – What does it mean?

- Now What? – What is the best response or next right action for this situation?

These are some of the best methods (and ones we consistently use ourselves) to wisely use the space between stimulus and response and not let fear and self-doubt dictate our reaction.

Intentionally deciding our responses with *purpose* and *intention* is a lifelong practice. We all have different sized gaps in our own space between stimulus and response. The key is to expand that space through practice and intention, so we use the time well.

It is important to understand how our conscious and unconscious perspectives may limit us. Knowing the following mindsets can help us use our time to be reflective and constructive in our response instead of reactionary.

1. **Critic**: When our inner-critic goes beyond helping us make good decisions, we can turn the critic on ourselves, creating *self*-deprecating thoughts, deprecating thoughts about *others* and

thoughts that *situations* will never be good enough.

2. **Perfectionist**: When we go beyond reasonably covering key details, we can repeatedly obsess over the same things that add no value and lack flexibility.

3. **Expert**: When we want to be right, strong, and get our way all the time, we do not collaborate well. Others find us overbearing, uptight and too set in our ways.

4. **Mechanical**: When we are primarily factual and logical, we do not continue to grow our adaptive, relational self, causing us to minimize our emotional connection with others and to seem disconnected.

5. **Helper**: When we put everyone's needs and wants before our own, we rob ourselves of our life by living others' lives.

6. **Pioneer**: When we lack *constancy of purpose* in our life and are constantly starting over and stopping what we do, our life and work is one big distracted churn causing focus and energy to dissipate.

7. **Victim**: When we are victims of life, we give our power away to others and life's circumstances, becoming in danger of learned helplessness.

8. **Ghost**: When we perceive that pain and things happen to us, we avoid welcoming life's circumstances and lean away from them instead of leaning into them for our disciplined growth and evolution.

Asking better and better questions can also help leaders get to root cause. Often, lack of or poor processes are at the root of performance issues. Knowing whether it is the person or process can help avoid future breakdowns.

One of the key aspects of leadership is knowing what processes are in place and ensuring that team members know what processes are in place. When team members aren't performing, often the first question asked of them is, *"Why did you do that?,"* or, *"Why didn't you do that?"* The results are that team members become fearful and anxious about their performance and their future.

If the leader understands that team member results will only be as good as the processes they are working in, the best question can be, *"Do you understand, and have you been taught the process?"* Leaders can now follow-up by asking if the team member can say what the process is so the leader can know if they're both on the same page and aligned on documented processes.

Take Action

For leaders, any time there is a performance issue, it is key to:

1. First, ask themselves, *"What is the process?"* or, *"Is there a process in place here?"* It is the leader's responsibility to ensure there are lean,

employee friendly work processes in place for all workflows.

2. Second, follow up with the team and ask them if they are aware of the process, and if they can repeat it back to you. Now, the leader knows what the person understands and has a better understanding of whether a process is in place and learned or if a process has simply not been followed.

3. Third, the leader now has two courses of action.

   - The person knows what the process is and did not follow it. The leader can now get a commitment from the team member that they do know the process and will certainly follow it next time. The team member explains what will be done differently in following the process.

   - The person didn't know the process. The leader now needs to share the process with the team member, ensure the individual is trained in the process and can demonstrate understanding by explaining and then following the process.

Either way, you now have an accountability commitment from the person, or the leader has awareness that there isn't a process in place and needs to work to create and implement an effective and efficient repeatable process.

Courageous Leaders **understand that they need to**
coach the person, not the problem **and** *fix the process,*
not the person.

People work in processes. As they follow
processes, the leader can offer up close and personal
leadership, reinforcing and celebrating with team
members as they provide the best service or products to
customers.

Leaders don't "blame-fix." They fix the work
process and coach team members who are working in the
process. This is the way leaders manage things (such as
processes) and lead people.

How Courageous Leaders Constantly Listen and Improve Communication

Communication is one of those buzzwords and something most everyone wants to work on and improve. There are shelves full of books on communication. How do **Courageous Leaders** constantly listen and improve communication?

Communication comes up with our clients all the time. People say their team members have communication issues or a CEO or President will say, *"I have communication issues with the people I'm responsible to lead."*

Whenever communication issues are presented as the problem, we visualize the word *communication,* and we put a big red **X** through it.

When we explore 'communication issues' with our clients, it really isn't about a communication problem. It is about disfunction, a lack of clarity, hesitation, fear and self-doubt.

When we need to discuss something, determining a very clear objective of what we will resolve is an important first step. What resolution do we really need here? Communication is just the vehicle for talking to each other to define the objective. A communication issue is often a lack of specificity around the objective— what needs to be worked out and worked through.

41

When we enter a conversation, we sometimes are dealing with high emotions and differing opinions. People talk to each other in ways that cause the conversation (the vehicle) to become more emotionally charged.

Sometimes, not meaning to, people will hit each other a bit below the belt in their comments. The conversation (the vehicle) becomes the objective and judging one another increases. The true objective and meaning of what the conversation is about is lost.

Take Action

Put an **X** through communication and get to the real objective and resolution by doing the following:

1. First, recognize that communication—verbal words, intonation and body language—is simply the vehicle for accomplishing an objective.

2. Second, determine the true objective of what we want to resolve or accomplish through each conversation. We want to be very, very clear on our objectives and what we want to accomplish. Now we can focus and stay in the conversation resolving something versus just having a wandering, superficial, emotional conversation.

3. Third, verify that we resolved what we wanted to resolve, or accomplished what we wanted to accomplish, based on the objectives we agreed on and that we stayed with the subject matter,

without letting the vehicle become the focus. How has our thinking grown and what actions will we and others now take?

If we understand and incorporate these three suggestions, we have a much better chance at using this vehicle (communication) to create mutual meaning, to reach resolutions, and to accomplish objectives.

With virtual communication becoming more prevalent, communication continues to be at the top of the list of challenges people face. Two parts of communication seem as important now as ever.

The first is better understanding how we communicate. People are often surprised by the small role words play in our communication. Research has broken it down as follows:[13]

- Body language – 55%

- Tone and speed of voice – 38%

- Words – 7%

Of the 7% communication we use in words, denotation (dictionary meanings) and connotation (personal meanings) of the words add tremendously to the possibility for miscommunication.

The denotative definition of a word could have dozens (even hundreds) of different possible meanings.

The word "go" for example has over 100 different definitions in the Oxford English dictionary.

Words also have connotative meaning on a national, cultural, organizational or even family level. These also include all the biases, lenses, and unconscious narratives we all have.

To improve communication, we must begin by agreeing collectively on what important words in our conversation mean. If we ask twenty people to define leadership, we may very well get twenty completely different answers.

A second part of communication that can be helpful is a better understanding of what is actually happening when we communicate. Communications researcher and author Dean Barlund created a model of six projected images that are present in any two-person communication[11].

1. The first is your own image of you speaking.

2. The second is your image of the person listening to you.

3. The third is an image of how you believe the other person is thinking and feeling about you as you speak (your projected self).

4. The fourth is the other person's self-image of herself or himself listening to you.

5. The fifth is the other person's image of you speaking to them.

6. The sixth is the other person's image of how they believe you may be thinking or feeling about them as you are speaking (their projected self).

These six images play off of each other and affect our communication in real-time. Both parties are constantly assessing their images of self, the other person, and their projected self during communication and making adjustments based on these assessments.

Take Action

Three actions leaders can take based on these concepts:

1. Awareness of the importance of factors other than words on communication. As a percentage, words are actually the least important part of a conversation.

2. Reflect the meaning (*not the words*) of what you believe the other person is saying based on their words, body language and intonation, as well as asking questions to check the assumptions being made during the conversation. We are making constant adjustments during a conversation based primarily on assumptions about the other person's body language and intonation. It is critical that important parts of the conversation aren't misinterpreted by these assumptions. Real-time feedback in the form of reflecting meaning

and asking clarifying questions can help limit these misinterpretations.

3. Ask for agreement on what was said and decided on during the conversation. People leave a conversation often with completely different interpretations of what was said and what was decided on. Checking before leaving a conversation can help limit the amount of misunderstanding.

The following quote by author George Bernard Shaw really sums up what often happens: *"The single biggest problem with communication is the illusion that it has taken place."*

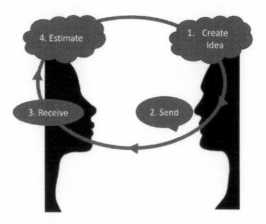

A simple example is to think about how many times people tell us about meeting someone, maybe for lunch, and they wait a long time, only to eventually find out that they went to different locations. Various versions of this example happen quite frequently!

Better awareness of self and others, better reflections and clarifying questions, and asking what the other person is taking away from a conversation can help remove some of that illusion. The great danger is that, without intentional verification, people believe whatever they want to believe based on what serves them best. Leaders know the wisdom of intentional verification and the danger of assumptions.

Chapter 3

Courageous Leaders Coach Others to Take the Next Right Action

The time for action is now. If not now, when?

How Courageous Leaders Help Everyone Be and See Themselves as Leaders

We believe in flipping so many of the old-timey, industrial-age concepts on their heads. Inverting the traditional organizational triangle is an example of one of these concepts. How do *Courageous Leaders* help everyone be and see themselves as leaders?

If everybody in the organization sees their leadership role as developing, supporting, getting the necessary training, removing barriers and providing resources for the team members they are leading, this parallel process takes effect throughout each level of the organization right up to customers.

Customer-Pulled | Employees-First

Parallel process begins with the way we view our role as a leader. We often talk about flipping the organizational triangle upside down, with the CEO on the bottom of the triangle and the customers on top with everyone facing upwards toward the customer.

In this type of environment, leaders listen to what team members need instead of just telling them what they need to do. Through parallel process, each level in the organization does the same for their reports.

When we're asking questions and getting feedback versus telling, the customer gets the best service or product. This is because we're seeking to understand what each person in the organization needs to be successful, including the customer. Leaders model these behaviors, actions and outcomes so their reports can do the same.

We had an owner of a business repeat to us what they've been telling one of their senior leaders, and we asked, *"Have you asked the person why they're not improving, why they're having trouble, and why they're making commitments over and over and not meeting those commitments?"*

We politely caught that in midair as the business owner was describing what they've been saying to the senior leader and was planning to say regarding what needs to change and how they should do it. What leaders need to remember is to *lead people and manage things.*

Our questions helped that business owner imagine the questions they could ask to allow the senior leader to do the work, to encourage them to think about why they were not meeting their commitments, and to figure out what was in their way, what they needed, and what they needed to do by when, rather than telling, telling, telling.

Asking is a real game changer. It helps leaders stay in their lane, and not go in others' lanes to do for them what they can do for themselves. Otherwise, we rob people the chance to learn by doing. This leads to "learned helplessness" in others.

Our coaching provides the opportunity for a parallel process of how leaders can ask questions instead of telling others what to do.

When people can tell and commit to their own story of what they will do, it will always be more powerful than a story someone else tells them.

It is the best way we know to develop critical thinking skills in others and to build cultures of self-accountability.

Asking, asking, asking instead of wanting to be helpful by telling, telling, telling. Leaders have way too much work of their own to hold onto doing for others' work and then complaining that they are too busy. Teach, coach and verify others have done their work to set standards and requirements. Leaders, work hard to stay in your lane!

With the best intentions in the world, trying to offer solutions or telling people how to do things can be a big detriment and a big roadblock in organizations. It creates cultures of dependence versus independence.

The leader's work is to empower people to be free to do their own work. That's when leaders create the power of the "multiplier effect." Highly developed individuals create highly developed teams, and highly developed teams create highly developed organizations producing benchmark performance.

The operating principle for leaders is, *"Never tell what you can ask!"*

When we talk about leadership, the character of any person leading is a key component of developing **Trust as An Operating System™**. Real leadership starts with caring, which is a key element of character. The toughest leaders are the most caring.

When we bring up the topic of caring, many leaders initially misunderstand what we mean by how leaders truly demonstrate caring for team members. We're not speaking of a mushy-gushy, touchy-feely, "soft skills." We believe that leaders get stuck in empathy and misunderstand *appropriate* vulnerability. This can be an enormous barrier for leaders.

True caring is about the *mission,* and it is tough. It involves believing in the potential of each team member to be successful in their role and standing in the space of that potential even when they don't see it for themselves. It is helping each person understand how they can continuously be successful and decide if their role is the best match for their *life-purpose* and skillset.

If the person cannot perform and deliver on the requirements of their job, or if there isn't alignment of their *purpose* with their work, the kind and caring thing for a leader to do is to quickly help them transition somewhere they can be successful, within or outside their current organization.

Take Action

Three key actions demonstrated by leaders who truly care:

1. **Helping each team member develop critical thinking skills to solve their own personal challenges and work solutions.**

   One of the primary roles of leadership is helping others enhance their critical thinking skills. This is all about the leader developing future leaders and how organizations grow and are sustainable over time. It is also a key aspect of organizational succession-development.

   Too often, leaders describe how people come to them with problems and leave with the leader's solutions. We hear many reasons why this happens. When we give answers before first exploring what the person can think of, we are on the path to codependency, which is the very opposite of critical thinking.

Helping a person develop critical thinking skills can be the greatest gift a leader can give.

2. **Standing in a place of possibility and believing in the potential of those you lead.**

To paraphrase a quote by author and poet Johann von Goethe, *"If you treat an individual as they are, they will remain how they are. But if you treat them as if they were what they have the potential to be, they will grow into that potential."*

> **If a leader doesn't believe a person has the potential to fulfill the responsibilities of their role, the kindest thing a leader can do is help the person find a place where they can thrive.**

Leaders consistently coach people, so they can find different and better ways to accomplish their *targets* and *goals*. If a person consistently cannot deliver, leaders who truly care about people and the *purpose* of the organization step right into these tough conversations to invest in helping people find a place where they can contribute and thrive. It is 100% an investment conversation. The leader is investing in the team member's (and the organization's) success. Caring does not mean stringing someone along under the guise of protecting them.

3. **Helping those you lead develop total *self-accountability*.**

   As people understand human nature and how people actually function in organizations, talk of "holding people accountable" disappears. Leaders who truly care about getting the best results for their organization, fulfilling its *purpose*, and unlocking the true potential of people they lead understand that self-accountability leads to sustainable progress.

   > **Trying to *hold people accountable* leads to temporary compliance. People develop self-accountability through consistent coaching by leaders to better understand and commit to fulfilling the *whys*, *hows* and *whats* that can help them be successful.**

True caring is not soft or easy. It is not a feel-good initiative to boost morale. It is a courageous, intentional way of being that can unlock the full potential of people, organizations and communities.

It all begins with leaders who truly care, are not afraid and know how to initiate and conduct investment conversations based on discussing what is going well and how each person thinks they can do even better. Next, each person makes a plan, commits to their plan, and engages in regular follow-up progress reviews with their leader.

When we discuss the true value that any leader really provides to their organization, many times it is a disorienting dilemma for leaders. They've gotten to a certain position based on their own knowledge and skills. We suggest the true value a leader adds is the following:

Doing only what other cannot do or be quickly taught to do.

Take Action

When we invert the organizational triangle (as we often talk about), the job of the includes leader the following:

- Hearing from *team members,* with crystal clarity, that *they* know how to be successful. They know the expectations, their role, their responsibilities and what results they will deliver. Until they can tell us (*not* us tell them), we cannot assume that they know.

- Developing each team member as a whole person. Leaders develop leaders. Managers train for tasks and jobs.

- Coaching people, not problems. Until people can transform themselves, they will continue to have the same and similar difficulties, just under different circumstances.

- Providing training for specific tasks and jobs. Leaders ensure people have the knowledge and skillset to take on the responsibilities of their job.

- Removing barriers. If the leader can knock down a wall for those they lead who cannot knock it down themselves, they do it.

- Providing available resources. If the **strategic direction** of the organization dictates increased resources, leaders obtain them for those they lead who cannot obtain it for themselves.

This is how a leader truly adds value: by doing only what others can't do and moving the organization forward to the next level of work that needs to be accomplished. When leaders get stuck in the doing, it's hard to stop doing and create the space for others to learn and do.

Leaders grow leaders and make time to:

- Step back.

- Gain more perspective.

- Gain different perspective.

- Think about and create a vision for the future.

Everything is in process. Nothing ever stays the same. Buddha is quoted as saying, *"Nothing ever stays the same. Everything's always changing."*

The leader must be very **strategic** in thinking about future direction:

- Where do we need to go next?

- What are the working relationships?

- How can I be more externally facing, making connections and being present in the community and in the region?

The leader can't do these things while also doing, doing, doing others' work.

The next question is, what development does the leader need to keep progressing?

We spend a lot of our time helping leaders realize they need to get out of the doing and not feel guilty and insecure about it. They mustn't think, *"If I give up my doing, will I still be needed?"* and instead, try to think, *"What will I be doing next to create and go to the future?"* That's often not very clear, highlighting the importance of the development of leaders.

Leaders developing and growing leaders means we're multiplying the capability of the organization. No one person regularly accomplishes great things alone.

It takes a lot of people to make the significant changes organizations need to be successful and competitive. Often, leaders find it a real hump to get over doing way too much and not delegating. We work with many leaders to get over this fear and to be secure with giving away more.

When we ask leaders the question, *"What is the true value you really add?"* or *"What's the only value you add?"* it usually takes a while for leaders to get to this answer: *"The true value I add as a leader is the work I do that no one else can do or work that I couldn't quickly teach them to do."* We love this part of our development with leaders.

Once leaders have the insight and bring themselves to act accordingly, they lead their organizations to the next levels of innovation, significantly improved performance and a promising future!

How Courageous Leaders Coach Team Members to Realize Unconscious Behaviors and to Imagine Different Outcomes

It is important that leaders become compassionate leader-coaches by coaching the person and not the problem. If we coach the problem, there will always be another problem, and the coachee will not transform. How do *Courageous Leaders* coach team members to realize unconscious behaviors and to imagine different outcomes?

- During a coaching conversation, we begin by deeply listening to the person we are with, reflecting back to them the meaning of what they are saying as best we can.

- We then ask questions with the intention of helping the person discover how they are currently being. This does not necessarily include what they are thinking or feeling, but *how* they are being.

- Finally, we ask them to imagine new ways they want to be in their story and what new ways they can work through the challenges they face.

A coaching conversation is all about the person being coached. As the coach, we become a thought-partner with the belief that each person has their own best solutions to work through any challenge they face.

One of the goals of our coaching with leaders is that they will be able to have better coaching conversations back in their own professional (and personal) environments. We strive to help organizations build coaching cultures, where everyone understands how to lead others through coaching conversations.

We often ask leaders how they think about sympathy, empathy and compassion as there are many definitions of each word. We think all three are a valuable part of the coaching process.

When we notice somebody isn't doing well, it can cause us to feel sad or sorry for the person. We want to help them do better. We see this as **sympathy**. If a leader becomes stuck in sympathy, they may see themselves as the "fixer" of others. They may spend their time fixing others' problems. With the best intentions, they may hold others back and create dependence versus independence.

When we think of **empathy**, we see it as moving from feeling sad for someone to taking on some of their feelings and better understanding how they may feel. The danger of empathy is getting stuck in someone else's feelings. We may lose objectivity or form a co-dependent relationship.

We define **compassion** as helping others discover the best ways to help themselves. It could be with specific challenges or developing themselves into the best self they can be, whatever that means for the individual. They may discover their best path isn't where they currently are, and this is a win for them and everyone else involved.

The process of moving from sympathy to empathy to compassion is shown below:

1. I hear you.

2. I understand what you're feeling (never exactly, but we all have similar feelings).

3. I care and will help you figure out the best way for you to help yourself.

Coaching parallels this process of moving from sympathy to empathy to compassion.

As leaders, people come to us with all sorts of challenges. Many can't see themselves in their story about their situation. Often, they will be the victim or the hero of their story. Part of coaching is helping people move away from the problem and focusing on themselves. As leaders, we are not solving problems but instead helping the person to see their role in the situation and to transform to a more strength-based self.

The leader-coach asks questions to help the person get beyond the "prison of their minds" to what it is that is causing the roadblock.

Questions help reveal possible lenses the person may not be able to see beyond or reveal something they cannot see within themselves. Often, our mind is just one big prison, limiting what we perceive and, in fact, limiting our whole life!

We can help the person understand their current reality, imagine a more desired reality and then ask them to come up with action steps to work toward the new reality. This process empowers the person to decide and commit to their own course of action and to improve their situation instead of giving their power away by being controlled by their circumstances.

Getting out of the problem and focusing on the *person* is fundamental to this process. We speak with wonderful leaders all the time, with all the good intentions in the world, who try to offer solutions and solve other people's problems. It feels good to help others and to solve problems for people.

The unfortunate consequence of problem-solving is that we create dependent people who keep coming back to us for answers. We have not uncovered what is actually causing their problem. Instead of developing independent people who have creative and critical thinking skills to solve their own problems, we condition people to be dependent on us to solve their problems.

The compassionate thing a leader can do is to remember the three components of the compassionate leader-coach:

- I hear what you are saying.

- I can empathize with what you are feeling because I have feelings too.

- I care enough to help you figure out the best way for you to help yourself.

After all, life is a series of challenges to be overcome. The question is, how can we best develop others' to be able to solve their own challenges? This is exactly how we and others grow, mature and evolve.

In any realm of development, as people become more, they can see more. As leaders develop themselves into better and better leader-coaches, they are able to guide team members to develop the critical thinking skills needed to be successful in life. We constantly work with *Courageous Leaders* who want to help their team members imagine different innovative outcomes.

Take Action

For leaders in organizations to be leader-coaches, they must first understand how to:

- Listen deeply while suspending judgements, solutions, and questions in their own mind.

- Reflect the *essence* of what the coachee is saying back to them. Reflections help the coach know they are on the right path and also help the coachee feel and know they are understood. We are not parroting words, but truly trying to capture the meaning of what the coachee is saying and not saying.

- Know when it is appropriate and necessary to move from listening and reflecting meaning to coaching.

The coaching process includes coaching others to see and understand:

1. How they are being in the situation (see themselves in their story).

2. How they would like to, want to or need to be in the situation (imagine a different way of being to achieve different results).

3. What action(s) they will need to take to create this new reality.

4. What barriers or resources are preventing or will prevent them from acting.

5. When the coach and coachee will meet to verify that what the coachee chose is working for them to create better results.

As with all development, coaching becomes a way of being. We become a leader-coach. It is not a step-by-step process that we consciously walk through. It is simply the best way we can become a leader-coach to develop those we lead.

Great leaders find joy and fulfillment in growing leaders. They are not threatened by fear and self-doubt as they grow others.

Leaders (and again, we are all leaders of our own lives) can use our Transformational Coaching Model™

to self-coach on any situation where there is an opportunity to transform ways of being.

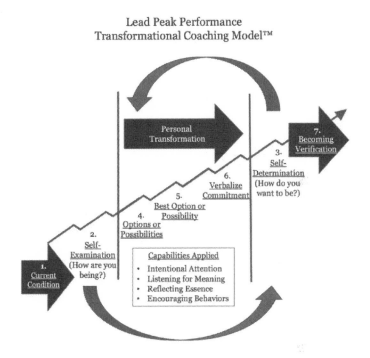

Lead Peak Performance
Transformational Coaching Model™

One question we hear repeatedly from leaders is, *"After coaching the person, how do I lead people who still aren't performing well."*

When we ask how long people have been with organizations and not performing well, we sometimes hear 5, 10, 15, even 40 years. Often no one can ever remember them performing well.

The reason many leaders give us for leaving people in a position when they are under-performing is the leader cares too much about the person and is hesitant to have a conversation with them about possibly transitioning to a position where they could perform at their highest potential.

Leaders initially tell us leaving a person in a position is done out of care for the person, but when we explore what's happening in the organization, we almost always find that everyone knows the person is out of season, including the person. The person generally isn't happy in that position, because no one wants to be somewhere they are consistently under-producing, and not only do they know it, but everyone else in the organization knows it as well.

The compassionate thing a leader can do is invest in and coach the person. This gives the opportunity for them to either perform or realize the best thing for them and the organization is to transition into a different position (within the organization or outside of it). It does not need to be a long and drawn-out process.

We often talk about *"seasons."* People are in season in an organization, and at times, people are out of season in an organization. As organizations change, some people are on board with the change and others aren't. The best thing for the person who isn't on board or is unwilling to change is to find a place where they are in season and can thrive, flourish, be happy and productive.

Leaders often take this on themselves, thinking that if they were a good leader, this person would perform. The leader believes the person's inability to perform is a reflection on their leadership and coaching.

Actually, the person is often just not in season for their current job responsibilities.

In these exceptional cases, it ends up becoming more about the leader thinking they are not good enough at leading rather than about the person, to the detriment of the leader and the person who is not performing. This is a subtle and unhealthy shift.

A thought we have when we're discussing this situation with groups or in individual coaching is, *"If this was someone I loved and cared about in this situation, and everyone including her knew she was out of season, but they kept her there while everyone talked about her, this would break my heart."* The compassionate thing to do is to help the person find the best place where they can be in season.

It is amazing when we ask leaders, *"Do you think you move too quickly or too slowly when people aren't performing?"* The answer is always, *"Too slowly."*

As a leader, it takes a lot of courage to put the effort into doing the best thing by that person, which, in these exceptional situations, is to help that person find their season somewhere else.

The key word is **courage**. The courage to step up and coach the person. If the person steps up and performs, that's a win. If the person realizes they aren't a fit and aren't in season so they move into another position in their organization, that is also a win, or if they move to a different organization or company, that is a win.

It is an act of courage and compassion to help someone make that step.

It breaks our hearts to see someone who is out of season not being helped to take their next step, sometimes to the outside. Acquiring new and additional proficiencies is not for everyone.

When there is a performance issue—people aren't getting along or something is not going well—we often hear about leaders missing this opportunity to step into a conversation versus not stepping in and hoping the issue will resolve on its own accord.

Being truly adept and effective at stepping into conflict conversations is something that takes intention and practice. This is also where the courageousness of the leader is demonstrated. The leader has to feel courageous and confident inside themselves to step into these conversations.

Ways leaders can effectively step into these conversations:

- Say what needs to be said. Sometimes it's just that simple—to say what needs to be said, clearly.

- Lead an environment that cultivates a culture of continuous improvement, always asking questions, talking about improvements, and asking how we can perform better.

Stepping into "investment conversations" isn't criticizing anyone. It is looking at how everyone can be more efficient and effective in their work so they can go home at night to their families feeling fulfilled and invested at their workplace and at home.

Developing team members to understand how to be more successful involves coaching them to better manage time. We often hear versions of the following comments:

- *"We need courses on time management."*

- *"We need better time-management skills."*

- *"Time management is a huge need."*

When leaders are stepping into conversations and asking, *"Are we using our time in the best way?"* they're really helping those they lead with time management. It's real and it's on-the-job improvement in time management.

It's not a criticism; it's leaders asking themselves, *"How do we constantly improve and become more efficient at managing our time?"* Then identify the next efficiency actions and implement them.

When leaders get out of their offices and go to Gemba[1], they learn a ton about work processes and

---

[1] Gemba is a Japanese term referring to the LEAN Kaizen practice of "going to where the work is."

whether the processes are employee-friendly, effective and efficient or if they need improvement.

In our experience, most work processes can be leaned out by 30-40%, yielding massive cost savings. Leaning out work processes involves reducing rework, defects, and redundancies and eliminating anything else that reduces efficiency. While all organizations desire savings, just imagine the amount of money left on the table each day!

Take Action

- Do the most important, long-term work early in the day before emails and meetings take over.

- Have a set time in the AM and PM to view and respond to email to avoid constant interruptions that derail concentration and progress. Each time we are interrupted, the best research reveals it takes about 20 minutes to get back in the flow of our work[10]. We tend to spend some time thinking about the last thing we dealt with before getting back in the flow of the work.

- Be more effective and efficient on phone calls and in-person meetings.

  o Begin with a cordial greeting.

  o Establish and accomplish the meeting objectives.

○ Summarize who owns the action items.

○ Wish people well and say, *"Goodbye."*

People pay a lot of money to go to courses on time management. A good leader can step into conversations right on the job. Leaders notice where time is being lost and ask, *"How do we manage our time much more effectively?"* The answer is always in the question!

How Courageous Leaders Coach Others to Turn Fear and Self-Doubt into Courage

The courage of the leader is something that comes up so often and there's much that could be said about it. How do *Courageous Leaders* turn fear and self-doubt into courage?

When do we need to have courage? It's when we fear something. That's when it's important to have courage, so that we can move beyond our fear. In fact, if there were no fear, there would be no need to have courage.

Fear shows up in our emotions as self-doubt, shame, worry, anger, resentment, depression, inferiority, superiority, greed, spitefulness, jealousy, loss, disempowerment, loneliness, lack of control. The base of all these feelings is loss.

If and when fear is not faced, understood, and acted on, our lives can become unmanageable. The good news is the opposite is also true. When we are aware of our fears and don't give them power, we can live our best life possible. The real question is what our fears tell us about what we need to deal with to create a better life instead of just running from them.

What we choose to proactively transcend is always our personal choice. What a test of our *Courageous Leadership* through life's unpredictable journey, which must be greater and more rewarding than a mind full of fear!

When courage is most needed, does fear have a taste? Many leaders tell us fear tastes like blood—it's that visceral. It comes when we are transforming fear and self-doubt into courage, and it happens in our heart. We've come to the conclusion that to have courage is to have heart. Our blood is still flowing instead of in a congealed state.

To not fail, we must not act only on what we're feeling. Instead, we have to move to what we're thinking. We cannot just act on feelings, because if we do, blood feels like it will congeal, and we won't have the courage and the heart to deal with and overcome the fear and self-doubt we generate.

Most of us struggle with indecision. Whether it's the fear of not doing the right thing or the fear of feeling uncomfortable, regardless of what the fear is about, we need courage and we have to have heart. Again, if there were no fear, there would be no need for courage.

We see situations where people just want everything to go along nicely and then find someone to blame when they don't. Sometimes, out of fear and self-doubt, people will "gaslight" and "ghost" others.

Take Action:

Several actions to take to be courageous in any condition:

1. Discover your best thinking.

Determine what is your best thinking at the present time and then act on that best thinking, not on thoughts causing feelings of anxiety and fear.

2. Live life on your own terms.

Decide what you think is the right thing to do based on everything you know, not based on what others think. Living to do the next right thing is a very courageous way of being. Others do not know the specifics of the situation as you do. You must have courage to act on your own knowledge of the situation, not out of weakness, fear and throwing others under the bus to save face.

3. Get away from negative thinking.

Stop the negative thoughts in their tracks. Stay with seeing a positive outcome and a positive end. Stay with those positive thoughts and don't become frozen from the fear of all the things that could go wrong. Vision a successful outcome.

4. Don't rehash the past

Rehashing the past robs us of our energy and our present. It distracts us from what we're trying to accomplish. It can really shake our confidence and shake our courage. We need to remember, we're a different person now than we were in the past. We've grown. We can't go forward looking in the rear-view mirror. What has happened has already taken place. It is only alive in our mind because we keep going over and over whatever happened.

5. **Always stay focused on** *purpose*

Ask:

- *"Why is it important to have courage in this situation?"*

- *"What is our **purpose**?"*

- *"What are we trying to accomplish?"*

- *"What's the **purpose** of the organization?"*

Staying ***purpose-focused*** at all times is "wise-living."

6. **Verify that decisions are courage-based**

Make sure to verify that your decisions are based on courage coming from your best thinking and a caring heart.

Focusing on what you and others do well and not spending so much time on weaknesses is another way to reduce negative stress.

There is so much to know in the world, and we all really know so very, very little. Why spend

so much time thinking about what we don't do well or aren't naturally good at doing?

As we work with leaders on development, one of the first questions we ask is for them to list all their strengths. There are many reasons why we do this, and one of them is that people don't take the time to think about their own strengths or to say them out loud.

Another reason we ask about strengths is, when leaders can intentionally focus on their own strengths, they have a better chance of noticing the innate strengths in others. They can point out the strengths of others in conversations, moving to more specific and meaningful feedback than generic "good job" and "nice work" compliments. They can also better position people to leverage their strengths.

Once leaders and team members identify their strengths, they are readily able to be clear regarding their next desired growth area.

Leaders constantly model the way to the next levels of Peak Performance. Perseverance, sheer mental and emotional grit, and resilience are necessary to get through the tough times of change. Leaders don't burden others with their own struggles. Others experience the leader's repeated strength and courage, helping them lead team members and their organizations to ever better Peak Performance.

Take Action:

Some key qualities that *Courageous Leaders* model in their own lives and are seen in places where they work include the following:

- Persistent focus despite the obstacles of change.

- Never considering themselves a victim.

- Avoid coming from fear and anxiety; not making their shortcomings another person's problem.

- Presenting their best self, not their own anxieties and difficulties.

- Licking their own wounds privately and not burdening others with them.

- Never throwing someone under the bus to save face.

Leaders repeat themselves through this positive modeling over and over, each time improving and evolving as they lead their organizations from Peak to Peak success!

The question for leaders is, how can they constantly repeat themselves with patience, determination and self-discipline, modeling the best in self accountability?

The leader must develop the mental, emotional and physical grit and resilience to do what needs to be done, so they can recognize and feel good about their accomplishments.

An important question for leaders to ask themselves every day is, *"What positive impact am I having on the people I'm leading?"* Positive work environments created by positive leaders remain at the top of employee satisfaction surveys each year. Negative relationships with supervisors continue to be the main reason people leave their jobs.

Take Action:

Questions for the positive leader to keep in mind every day:

- What *energy* am I bringing and how does my *energy* impact and *influence* people around me?

- Who do I need to be to encourage my own and others' best thinking and best efforts?

- What difference will I make this day in the lives of others?

Creating a positive, inspiring and reinforcing work environment where people take pride in doing their best work results in delivering the best products/services to the customer. This is one of the most important roles of leaders as they lead people, teams and organizations, even during the toughest times, to progress from one level of performance to the next level of Peak Performance.

Chapter 4

Courageous Leaders Create
Diverse Cultures of Innovation

*The open, curious mind seeks constant improvement
and growth.*

How Courageous Leaders Invite, Value and Honor Diversity

Research and experience prove over and over again that the more diversity represented on a team, the more innovative the team can be. How do *Courageous Leaders* invite, value and honor diversity?

Endless types of diversity abound: ethnicity, race, gender, sexual-preference, age, birth location, education, and so on.

We believe that innovation is the lifeblood of any organization. Diverse teams delivering superior solutions, products and services to their customers.

This reality has been demonstrated much longer than we have been alive. How do *Courageous Leaders* invite, value and honor diversity?

Every day, we get to the transformative experience of bringing diverse voices to a table to learn and grow with by valuing and including all experiences, points of view and ideas.

Observing people as they truly hear each other and watching them see the world through new eyes is life-changing for us as much as it is for the people we work with. We get to watch people discover lenses and biases they were unaware of before our group dialogues. They become aware of, for the first-time, old records that have been spinning in their heads, repeating old scripts that have been passed down for generations along with old rules that limit growth.

People tell us they have changed their conversations with their families at the dinner and breakfast tables. They are breaking old cycles of negative thinking and hidden stereotypes that have distorted their view of the world.

People tell us how much this work has changed their own and their family's lives in positive ways. People think differently, speak differently and even vote differently.

We truly believe that this is some of the most important work we do and that it has a chance to positively impact the world.

We hear all the time how difficult it is for most people to incorporate new learning into daily life. There is always potential for people to progress and grow through the challenges and opportunities they face. For thousands of years, philosophers, teachers, spiritual-figures and storytellers have provided lessons and examples of how to live a life of growth, meaning, joy and continuous-development.

Unfortunately, we often fall back into old ways of being as soon as the challenging situation has passed. This really speaks to the core difference between development and training.

When we go through training (which is from the outside in), we are usually given instruction of some sort on how to do some task or specific job. Hopefully the trainer is knowledgeable about the topic and delivers instruction in a way we understand. At the end of the training, we have new knowledge and skills that we can apply to our work or to other areas of life.

Development, on the other hand (which is from the inside out), is an opportunity to change the way we see and experience the world around us. It is a chance to explore the lenses we experience life through and to see the world with new eyes. Writer and philosopher Dr. Wayne Dyer said, *"When we change the way we look at things, the things we look at change."*

Development gives us the chance to change and to use any challenge or obstacle as a way to grow and develop.

The four components of development:

1. Begin with an idea or concept. We like to use "disorienting-dilemmas" to begin a conversation.

2. Each person goes inside to determine how they think and feel about the idea.

3. Through facilitated group dialogue, use collective-intelligence to imagine and create new or different ways of understanding the idea, problem or opportunity to be solved to gain a larger perspective or a more holistic truth.

4. Incorporate this new way of understanding into daily life practices. In this way, we are constantly growing and becoming more and better, creating more value in our life and work.

So, why is it so difficult for people to develop and change the way they experience the world? As we're learning new ways of being, our ingrained habits are constantly trying to pull us back to how we've always been and what we've always done. The majority of our thoughts each day are almost *exactly the same* as the day before. Our brain loves to conserve energy through repetition.

In the second step of the development process described above, it is critical that we've developed cognitive and emotional hooks to our new learning. When we're working with groups, if we hear people haven't been able to incorporate the development into their daily lives, the reason is often that either a strong cognitive or an emotional hook hasn't been established.

People need to really desire the change both logically and emotionally if they are going to put the needed effort and energy into changing. We discussed in a previous chapter the Ancient Greek understanding of influencing others, and it applies here to influencing positive and sustainable growth.

Pathos is the emotional hook to the idea or concept. Until somebody is moved on an emotional level about a new way of feeling about a concept, idea or a cause, new habits and ways of being will not be incorporated.

Logos is the cognitive hook to the idea or concept. Does the new way of thinking make sense to the logical/rational portion of the brain? Until there is a cognitive hook to the idea or concept, new habits and ways of being will not be incorporated and integrated into our practice of how we lead and live.

We believe in the potential of human beings to grow, develop and change. We have the privilege to watch people develop and live new ways of being. They see the world through new eyes and achieve results they never imagined were possible.

The leadership responsibility is to continue to facilitate this change and to encourage people to invest in the development of those they lead. The potential is there; we just need to unlock it and, as leaders, we must never "blink" or hesitate on the commitment to enable others to become their best possible selves.

How Courageous Leaders See Conflict as Positive and Use It as Fuel for Growth

We often hear about the difficulty people have with what they perceive to be conflict conversations. We believe that some of our best work is helping people view conflict in a different way.

People usually think of conflict as a negative thing. We hear terms, such as *constructive-criticism, conflict-resolution, crucial-conversations*, and *tough conversations*. How do **Courageous Leaders** see conflict as positive and use it as fuel for growth?

We like to flip this entire way of thinking about conflict on its head. We think about these tough conversations as positive conflict.

We encourage people from this day forward to engage only in investment conversations and to never again have another hard conversation that everyone dreads having.

There will always be conflict in the world. People have different ideas, different views and different beliefs. Conflict is as sure to occur as the sun coming up every morning. The question is, do we see it as negative or as positive?

When there is conflict or tension, this is a wonderful opportunity to stop and say to ourselves, *"We're having this conflict because we care about the topic or issue."*

It is also a wonderful opportunity to see the world through someone else's eyes and to ask very curious questions. Instead of saying, *"This is the way I see it,"* and the other person saying, *"Well, this is how I see it,"* and getting into a vicious ping-pong match, we can realize the opportunity to see the world in a way that we couldn't before.

Some say that all positive change comes through conflict, and the absence of conflict is where the lowest common denominator in negative situations remains or grows. We either step forward into growth or step back into comfort and safety. Often, we unconsciously do the latter.

We work with leaders to not be fearful of or step away from conflict but leverage it as a wonderful opportunity for improvement. Conflict will always be a reality because we all have different perceptions.

Change is another form of conflict. People dislike change because it upsets their homeostasis. By thinking about change as improvement, we remove the negative connotation that comes with the word "change."

Unless we're changing just for the sake of changing, what we're always doing is working to continuously improve one thing after the other. We become *improvement-agents* instead of *change-agents*. The leader can help people see conflict for what it actually is: an opportunity and a call to build better relationships and to improve work systems, products and services.

If we're truly investing in people, we want to help them grow as much as possible. Conflict becomes a big positive because it is an investment in another human being. We need to truly care about someone enough to have these investment conversations and to understand the opportunity for growth.

Many people avoid needed conversations because they don't want to hurt someone's feelings. Or they simply don't know how to give difficult feedback. The question is, *"What is in the best interest of the other person and the organization?"* We observe so many people being hurt because their leader isn't investing in them using clear, caring language.

People need to know how to grow as a stronger and stronger performer. When we hear someone say, *"I'm going to have a very difficult conversation today and I've been dreading it,"* we explore this with them. Often we find they are having a conversation with someone about something that person can do better. We think some of our best work is when we have leaders think of it not as a difficult conversation but what it truly is—an *investment conversation.*

We hear of the old-school terms such as the "sandwich approach" (say something positive, then negative, then positive), constructive-criticism and conflict-resolution. However, the research and studies conclude that these old-school approaches do not work. People will focus solely on any real (or perceived) criticism in a negative light, become defensive and even shut down.

Criticism is criticism. Whether you put it in a nice sandwich with lettuce and tomatoes doesn't make any difference. It's criticism and people feel and react to the criticism biologically and chemically.

If it's an investment conversation, the leader recognizes everything the person does well (because we can only go forward) and then helps the person gain awareness by thinking of ideas to perform even better.

This point of view changes how both feel about the conversation. The leader doesn't have to think they are having a *difficult conversation*. The leader can think about having an *investment conversation*. Experiencing this conversation as an investment is pretty exciting.

It has to be real. This isn't changing some words around to manipulate people. It is truly caring for another human being and seeking wins for them, the organization and the *mission* of the organization. When done in an authentic way, in a manner that is truly an investment, what greater gift can you give someone?

We're either investing or criticizing. It's really just one or the other. Performance and results speak for themselves. Organizations where people feel invested will outperform organizations where people feel criticized.

Change is inevitable. The universe is changing and constantly expanding. The research is too clear and compelling to ignore. If we are not constantly and intentionally evolving ourselves, our teams and our organizations, we begin to fall out of season. If we are not renewing and growing, we begin to decay. Change is not always good or bad. Life is change, and we are empowered to decide how we deal with it and how we lift others to understand the positive and natural life-giving force of change.

How we frame change in our own mind and then articulate change to our teams will determine whether we are adding stress or breathing life into ourselves, the people we lead and our organizations. If we don't help those we lead understand the positive nature of change or if we ourselves view change as a negative thing, we live in and create an environment of stress and fear. If we view change as empowering us to constantly improve and grow, we breathe life into those we lead. Instead of change-agents, we become improvement-agents with a growth mindset to grow ourselves, others and our organizations.

Take Action:

As improvement-agents and lifelong learners, we can ask ourselves the following questions:

- Am I, the people I lead, and the people in my organization tired and stressed or alive with light in their eyes?

- Do I regularly reinforce the idea of continuous improvement in all aspects of business and life in a positive and uplifting way?

- Am I at peace with the universe, understanding that change is constant, and the way we see it and embody it can be an empowering choice?

- Do I continue to gain the best insights by listening to team members to learn what they need to best serve their internal and external customers?

- Am I reading books and articles, listening to podcasts or audiobooks, or watching Ted Talks and other videos to stay on top of the latest trends and research in my field and in leadership?

- Is my spirit *ignited* by the idea of growing and expanding my awareness and insights, and then behaving and acting on what I have learned?

- Am I consistently grateful for what is in my life?

Leaders can only lead others as far as they're able to lead themselves. If leaders are not courageously improving themselves, they will cap the potential of their teams and entire organizations.

What is often perceived as a negative situation can be turned into a positive outcome by the leader who is confident in conflict. Conflict is natural and necessary for growth. Just as a wildfire helps nourish the soil and prepare it for new seeds to take root, conflict is an opportunity for the leader to prepare teams for the seeds of new growth.

Below are examples of potentially negative situations that can lead to positive action through confident conflict:

- A team member listens carefully to an irate customer, takes notes and later discusses improvement opportunities with their team. The customer has given direct insight into an improvement opportunity. The conflict presented by the customer can be turned into positive action. In fact, customer complaints are "precious knowledge." Those complaints tell us exactly what needs improvement.

- A leader has a confrontation and coaches a volatile employee on their lack of production due to habits of negative self-talk, gossiping and creating drama on their team. The conflict is actually an investment, initiated by the leader, which can generate new awareness and insight for the team member. Where other supervisors have avoided this conflict, the leader who is confident in conflict understands that growth and improvement are not possible without making necessary, clear investments in others.

Planes take off into the wind, using the energy created by the wind to their advantage. Conflict is energy that can be used for investment and positive outcomes. A leader who understands the necessity and positive nature of conflict can lead their team and organization to Peaks of Performance far beyond those who are conflict averse.

If we proactively and consistently embody and verbalize the positive nature of continuous improvement, we can help our teams and organizations stay in harmony with universal change and thrive in it.

The real question is, *"How courageous is the leader?"*

How Courageous Leaders Create Diverse and Inclusive Cultures of Innovation

Earlier in this chapter, we discussed some of the many types of diversity. Our natural energy is yet another type of diversity we can discuss. How do *Courageous Leaders* create diverse and inclusive cultures of innovation?

As leaders continue their development journey, natural energy and energy preferences become another type of diversity to look for. Of course, these energy preferences do not limit us in any way. Each of us can flex and excel in any of these if the *purpose* of our work is strong enough. People often naturally gravitate more to one of the following four areas:

1. **People who naturally think in terms of helping and doing the work.**

    Some people are very task-oriented. They are very aware of the rules and the regulations and keep things on track. They often naturally excel at seeing the *vision* of the organization and pulling the team to the *vision*, consistently accomplishing *goals* and *targets*. We say people with this type of natural energy are the helpmates of the organization.

2. **People who naturally think in terms of** *purpose* **and** *mission.*

    Some people are naturally drawn to the *mission* and *purpose* of the organization. They can see the

97

purpose of the organization in every area of their work, and it matches their *self-purpose*. We say people with this type of natural energy are the soulmates of the organization.

3. **People who naturally think in terms of processes and systems.**

Some people see the systems and processes (or lack of them) in everything. They can tell where a process is missing or isn't operating efficiently. They can see the system or process that can correct so many of the errors or the deficiencies in their own life and in any organization. We say people with this type of natural energy are the mindmates of the organization.

4. **People who naturally bring fun and levity to the workplace.**

Some people naturally bring fun and levity to the work. They make work more enjoyable. When conversations get too serious, they lighten the mood and the spirit of others. This can provide a breath of fresh air and more realistic and positive perspectives. We say people with this type of natural energy are the playmates of the organization.

Inclusive environments value and leverage the strengths of people who excel in each of these four energy dimensions.

- **Helpmates** ensure things stay on task, deliverables are met, and rules and regulations are adhered to. (The planes run on time.)

- **Mindmates** ensure systems are in place that people can work in most efficiently. (The planes are designed with maximum efficiency and effectiveness.)

- **Soulmates** ensure the organization is *mission-focused*, and people are inspired by their work. (There is a deeper and bigger reason why it is important to create the planes in the first place, for example, connecting families to each other or delivering lifesaving equipment.)

- **Playmates** ensure there's some natural levity and fun on the teams and people enjoy their work and working together as friendly colleagues. (An example would be the flight attendants on Southwest making flights humorous and fun for passengers.)

The opposite is true when we find any of these four strengths missing in organizations:

- Without helpers and doers, people may have great processes and inspiring work they enjoy, but they may not meet deliverables, achieve Peak Performance and properly follow rules, requirements and regulations in a disciplined, orderly fashion.

- Without systems and processes, everyone may be working hard, *mission-pulled* and having some fun, but not in an efficient and effective way.

- Without *purpose* and *mission*, everyone may be working hard in efficient processes, enjoying their work, but lacking inspiration and motivation to do their work at *Peak Performance*.

- Without the fun and levity people, everyone may be focused on the *mission*, working hard in proper systems and processes, achieving tough *goals*, but not enjoying their work. Everybody's very serious, the work is not enjoyable, and people don't easily relate to and support one another.

Recognizing the strengths in others, and hiring people, promoting people, and putting people in positions where they can best leverage their strengths, can go a long way in balancing an organization and achieving peak levels of performance.

Another example of diverse energy is **convergent and divergent energy**. On a team, it's really important to have both.

- **People who want to converge** – They desire closure, want to implement and move to action quickly.

- **People who want to diverge** – They prefer to discuss different options before implementing and not converge as quickly.

To those who like to converge, diverging can be maddening. A team may have talked about something or vetted an issue, and just when the team is ready to pull together, a team member who prefers to diverge will say:

- *"You know, I think there's one more thing."*

- *"We may have missed this."*

- *"Is there a better option?"*

And the team goes, *"Ugh! We thought we were there. We thought we were converging."*

This diverging team member (or several team members) is important in terms of diversity. For those who converge, they will want to vet, think, pull together and come to a solution. They give this idea or this solution attention, attention, attention. This idea, solution or opinion—whatever they give attention to—just gets bigger, bigger, bigger.

From a leadership perspective, this leads us to ask, what is orbiting this answer or this solution? There are other considerations. There are other possibilities. There may be another answer, even another solution or other pieces, but the fact is, those who like to converge on a project, on a solution, or on anything are going to give attention to the solution, to what seems obvious.

Instead of judging and being impatient, valuing divergent thinkers can lead to breakthrough ideas. Without diverging team members, teams risk missing all the other considerations and important parts of any solution that are orbiting around. If we don't see and intentionally give attention to these other pieces that are orbiting around the answer, we may miss pieces to the answer. We become too focused on just one part of the answer because we only focus on one aspect of the problem/opportunity.

Leaders must listen for and invite divergent team members to contribute.

- *"What other possibilities are orbiting around this solution?"*

- *"What are other pieces we should consider?"*

- *"Is there one more thing?"*

- *"Shouldn't we consider this?"*

These questions are what the divergent thinker is thinking about. There is value in this form of diversity. We don't converge too quickly, and we don't diverge forever, but we get this very critical complement and balance. Requiring balance through diversity of perspective and voice is the true work of the leader.

This one example describes how diversity of approach enables teams not to leave the best solutions and performance on the table—a crucial competitive advantage!

Chapter 5

Courageous Leaders Ignite the Full
Potential Within Others

*The best practice is being on track and staying on track
regardless of the circumstances... Being among it, but
not of it.*

How Courageous Leaders Find the Resilience and Grit to Lead Through Difficult Times

Based on our experience and research, we believe that one of the most important attributes of a leader is having an indomitable spirit. This raises an important question about how *Courageous Leaders* find the grit and resilience to lead through difficult times.

We have such a deep belief about an indomitable spirit, and there are many attributes of an indomitable spirit. One aspect that deserves our attention is *discipline*. The disciplined self is the powerful self.

Take Action:

When we think of the disciplined leader as an attribute of an indomitable spirit, there are three actions that leaders can take:

1. Determine what degree of achievement is necessary next in their own self, in their business or in their organization. What is the upper limit of the achievement, and what is the lower limit of the achievement that is appropriate for the time and the people to move the organization forward?

2. Create the action steps to be taken; who needs to be involved in each phase of the plan? Diversity of perspective and thought is golden for innovative thinking and actions. It is truly our life resilience and *GRIT!*

3. Determine what timeframe is appropriate for this amount of achievement that is within our upper and lower limits. We don't want the timeframe to be too short or too long. So, the second question is, what is the timeframe we are thinking of making for this level of achievement?

4. Have the mindset of no excuses – living an excuse-free life. We're moving forward with a certain amount of achievement within a certain time period. The question becomes, *"If things don't go well, or if there are errors, how quickly do we intervene, change or go in a different direction?"* There are no excuses for not meeting our achievement **goals** on time, so we must act quickly with intention on our path to change it and to make it appropriate, so we deliver on our achievement within the time we said we would. It becomes time-bound, just as in life.

These four action steps come right to mind when thinking about developing the self-discipline needed to lead with an indomitable spirit and to lead an excuse-free life. In fact, life is a time-bound improvisational experience, a meaningful and worthy journey that daily invites our best selves.

When leaders are inconsistent, and when we don't know what to expect from them or what mood they may be in, team members spend time and energy trying to predict how to engage with them. Bad moods are super contagious. They spread like wildfire. We think about this as the "weather" we bring to others.

Courageous Leaders continue to better understand how contagious their presence is, and they become more aware of the weather they bring.

The leader who is inconsistent and unpredictable becomes a wildcard factor. Research puts the number of people who have a high level of self-awareness at 6-8%. If leaders aren't constantly working on self-awareness and intentionally choosing what energy to bring to every situation, there will be a wildcard factor going on all the time.

If we don't understand the impact we are having on others based on choosing the energy we bring, the amount of ***influence*** we have diminishes and may even be lost.

We talk about weather analogous to presence. What weather are we bringing when we walk into the room? Can people predict our weather? Are people grabbing umbrellas before we even say a word just based on our body language?

To have consistency, we're really talking about repeated behaviors and repeated practices. It's hard to get consistent performance unless you have a consistency of repeated emotionally regulated behaviors and practices.

When we think of consistent performance, we begin with each person being a little better in their performance each day, leading to a team being a little better in its performance and then an organization being a little better in its performance.

Repeated day after day, these actions add up. Each time something is carried out, if it could be a little better (research says around 3 percent), over time this is what makes good companies great companies, and great companies exceptional companies, and on and on.

Take Action:

There are a few things we can all do to have this repeated excellence in performance:

1. **Self-accountability to *goals*** – Personal, for the team, and for the organization, and helping reach those *goals* personally and for the organization. No one else holds me accountable. We're 100 percent self-accountable for the *goals* that we're trying to reach.

2. **Consistent thinking** – Not being pulled off track by all self-doubts, fear and distractions. Keeping focus and having consistent thinking about our own accountability as we move toward the *goals*.

3. **Consistent behavior** – If we have more consistent thinking, we're going to have more consistent, regulated, disciplined behaviors.

4. **Consistent performance** – Those consistent disciplined behaviors are going to lead us to consistent performance to reach our necessary or desired *goals*.

5. **Verify** – Self-evaluation, evaluation of how each person on the team has performed, evaluation of the team as a whole and evaluation of how the organization has performed. By going back and having this consistent evaluation, we're able to tweak, improve and enhance our accountability for successful enhancements.

It's our thinking about what's desired and what we are trying to achieve, our accountability for our behaviors leading to a regular pattern of behaviors, and constantly making the adjustments and changes needed that will move great performance to enhanced excellence every single day.

In fact, we can liberate and free ourselves to accomplish the mindset and success we wish for ourselves each day. Happy, satisfied, and peaceful individuals don't *have* a great day; they *make* **it a great day every day!**

How Courageous Leaders Inspire Increased Engagement in Meaningful and Enjoyable Work.

Engagement in work continues to remain at around 30% year after year according to the annual Gallup Employee Engagement Poll[12]. We work with leaders in many ways to help improve this dismal number. How do *Courageous Leaders* inspire increased engagement in meaningful and enjoyable work?

The importance of understanding the *whys, the hows, and the whats* is one way we work with leaders to help create and maintain engaging environments.

The *Whys*:

It begins with leaders asking *why* questions. These are not accusatory *whys*, such as, *"Why did you do that?"* or, *"Why didn't you do that?"* The *why* questions should help connect the topic of conversation to the bigger *purpose* of the organization beyond the task at hand. Often, the question to connect the task to the greater *purpose* of the organization is, *"Why do you think this is important given our mission?"*

An example we hear is that the leaders we work with are often tasked with informing team members of new policies or regulations. This assignment often leaves team members feeling like more work is being added to their day with no clear reason or that they have less authority and autonomy to make decisions.

Asking *why* questions to help team members connect the new policy or regulation to the greater *purpose* of the organization or thinking about why the policy may have been put in place to begin with, can help team members see beyond the annoyance of another rule or regulation.

One of the most powerful forces in the world is when a person's *mission* in life is aligned with their organization's *mission*. An essential part of leadership is helping each team member connect their personal *purpose* (their *mission*, their *why*) to the organization's *purpose* (the organizations *mission*, its *why*).

The connection of personal and organizational *mission* may not always be 100% direct. We worked with a leader in sales who struggled to find alignment of her *why* with her organization's *why*. She wanted to positively impact people and make a positive difference in the world. Selling insurance was not fulfilling her *mission*. She wondered if she should change careers to find this alignment somewhere else.

She finally realized that she could make a positive difference in the lives of each member of those she led on her team (her internal customers). These were mostly people fresh out of college in their first jobs using their degrees. She could have a huge impact on these people's lives and first career experience. This aligned with the organization's *mission* to deliver exceptional customer service. By focusing on lifting each team member, she helped them do the same for the customers.

In addition to the big *why*, the *why* in each interaction with team members (and customers) is also critical in creating and maintaining engaging work environments. It has been said, *"We judge ourselves by our intentions; we judge others by their actions."*

We know our intention (the reason *why* we say and do what we do). If others do not know our intentions (the *why* behind our actions and words), they are left to guess.

Again, research continues to support that about 80% of our thoughts are negative or concerning. We are biologically programmed to think negatively for safety and survival. Unfortunately, this wiring also plays into how we interpret other's intentions when they are not made clear. If people are left to guess at another person's intentions, they often will naturally assume the negative. Ensuring others know our good intentions (the *why* behind our decisions and actions) is an important part of improving employee engagement.

The *Hows*

How we think and feel about a situation affects our communication. Our behaviors, actions, tone and body language reveal *how* we really think and feel, regardless of we say.

Since we want people to be more engaged in their work, it is important to pay attention to our feelings and moods and the effect they have on our interactions. Being intentional about our thoughts can positively affect *how* we communicate. Increasing employee engagement demands that the leader is consistently in control of their thoughts and emotions. Often, team members are not upset about what is said, but about *how* the message was delivered.

Coaching helps team members examine ways they are being that may be holding them back. Often they may have little awareness. Helping team members establish *how* they are being and *how* they want or need to be is the objective of transformational coaching.

How an organization conducts business is also important in creating engaging environments. Check if everyone is in alignment on the following:

- *How* to best serve customers.

- *How* to handle a customer complaint.

- *How* their job needs to be performed.

Teams developing and agreeing on key operating principles and behaviors helps everyone align to agreed-upon ways of working together.

The *Whats*

If we've established *why* we do what we do and *how* we'll do it, the remaining factor is a clear understanding and alignment of *'what* we are doing. Often, team members in organizations we work with express frustration in not knowing exactly *what* they are trying to accomplish.

A clear ***vision***, ***objectives*** and measurable ***goals*** are needed to achieve an alignment of *what* team members are working to accomplish within the organization. Each team member must know what their deliverables are, and what they need to do (and not do) to be successful.

Clear expectations, clear roles and responsibilities and clear ways of being successful are examples of the *whats* that help team members feel in control of and become accountable for their own success.

When we begin with aligning the organization's *why* with each team member's *why*, and then establish *how* team members will behave while conducting business and, finally, align *what* everyone is trying to accomplish, we have an organization with an engaging environment.

Hiring is the first step in this process. If we fail to hire, retain and promote for alignment of the *whys* the *hows* and the *whats*, we may end up with an organization that mirrors the national average of only 30% employee engagement. ***Courageous Leaders*** must turn this pathetically low percentage upside down, and we have the perfect energy to do just that.

How Courageous Leaders Recognize and Develop Their Political and Administrative Capabilities

Understanding the difference between administrative and political capabilities and the leader's strengths and preference toward one or the other is essential. How do *Courageous Leaders* recognize and develop their political and administrative capabilities?

The **political-self** (of course we're not thinking about the political arena in the world) asks, *"How strong are my relationships, and how well do I relate to people?"* and, *"Where can we take the organization next, how fast, and how well?"*

The political side of the leader is made up of their relationships with people and how well they relate to each person. No one person can consistently accomplish great things alone. The **political-self** inspires shared *vision*, engagement and self-accountability in those they lead.

The political-self thinks about every interaction and asks:

- Am I enrolling people in what we need to accomplish?

- Are they becoming supportive of the next distance they and the company can go and the legacy that we can leave in this organization or company?

115

- How many are supporters?

- How many have enrolled?

- How many are on board?

- Have I had any interactions that will create adversaries (people who are not on board, people who are going to push against the direction that we need to go)?

- How will I be able to get them on board?

The **administrative-self** asks, *"Do we have everything lined up in terms of the **vision**, action plans and resources?"*

The administrative side of the leader makes sure whatever we've imagined, with the support we've gained, is brought into reality. The **administrative-self** will determine whether or not we have a very elegant implementation. Leaders have not led until results are a reality.

The administrative-self asks:

- What does the needs analysis show?

- What is the plan?

- What are all the achievement *objectives* of the plan?

- Who is involved in the plan?

- How fast is the plan going to move?

- What's going to be done by when?

- What are going to be the procedures and processes?

- What tools and resources do we need?

- What are the **goals**, result **measures**, **targets** and **timeframes**?

- When will be the debrief of results verification?

We have to pay careful attention to both our **political-self** and our **administrative-self**.

Without the **administrative-self**, strong political leaders may have formed wonderful **visions**, relationships and engaged teams, but when they say, *"Ok everybody, let's go!"* the people ask, *"What is my role and how do we execute and implement the vision?"* Otherwise, the **vision** is just a wish and a dream.

Without the **political-self**, strong administrative leaders may have the best **strategy** and plans, but when they say, *"Ok everybody, let's go!"* they look around and no one is there.

Of course, if we aren't particularly strong in the **political-self** or the **administrative-self**, then we need to promote, hire or partner with someone who can balance and complement our strengths. Leaders hire in areas where they aren't as strong. As is often said, a balanced life is a really great life—so it is at home and at work!

Chapter 6

Courageous Leaders are Easy to Love and Hard to Please

Set and reach high standards while holding people close.

How Courageous Leaders Become Easy to Love and Hard to Please

In our development work with groups, we often present what we call a **disorienting dilemma,** and we facilitate dialogue encouraging and using collective intelligence to help transform ways of thinking about a topic or idea. How do *Courageous Leaders* become easy to love and hard to please?

Easy to love and hard to please are such important leadership attributes! We try to imagine the best leaders we've ever known who cause us to say, *"I love working with that leader!"* After further conversation, people tell us the best leaders they've experienced also had very high expectations. Their leader was hard to please because they held such high standards.

When we talk about this kind of leader, the high expectations, or *hard-to-please* part, is as much about each individual living into their own full potential as it is any other result. This leader stands in the possibility of how far each person can grow and holds that space.

It isn't about pleasing the leader; it's about each person stretching themselves and not being pleased with anything less than their personal best. People often remember a teacher who may have been very tough on them, but they knew the teacher cared deeply about them and their success as an individual.

This kind of leader also has very high adaptive abilities (*easy to love*):

- Being gracious, giving and other-focused.

- Caring and interested in other people's lives, wanting them to do well.

- Wanting to lead each person in the organization based on who that person is.

- Wanting to have their organization function based on how human beings best function - the science of human behavior.

This leader also has very high standards and expectations (*hard to please*):

- ***Objectives, measures*** and due dates that are clear.

- Work processes that are employee-friendly.

- Team members know exactly what they are expected to deliver to reach the organization's evolving ***vision***.

- Team members knowing exactly what they're working to accomplish to reach the organization's ***vision***.

- The leader's expectations are consistent and in alignment with the organization's ***objectives***; there is no guesswork.

- There is nothing vague about expectations, and team members are getting performance feedback all the time through conversations, as well as through weekly or bimonthly work sessions and regular supervision.

Not only is the leader hard to please, but people become hard to please about themselves, meaning they take high self-accountability.

Yes, the leader is *hard to please* with the best intentions *for* those they lead. They see the best in people and stand in areas of potential. People growing as human beings and growing their ability to deliver better and better results is the best form of job security.

We discuss the leader's **vision** being a stretch for people versus a strain on people. The **stretch goal** produces the creative tension that helps team members find innovative ways to continuously move themselves and the organization forward. How does this factor into being easy to love and hard to please?

Every decision we make and every **objective** (what we need to accomplish) we're working on moves us towards that **vision**. This helps us with all decision making. Is a decision just chasing the shiny penny of the day, taking us sideways and not toward the **vision**?

With the creative tension the **vision** provides and **objectives** that are very clear, people can:

- Take ownership.

- Be self-accountable.

- Be proud to deliver on what they and the team are responsible for in pursuit of the *vision.*

Easy to love (*easy to work with*) and hard to please (*high standards*) is a disorienting dilemma and is key to excellent leadership performance. With this kind of leadership, you are growing team members, growing teams, and growing organizations.

The *vision* is always evolving, and what we need in order to accomplish it is always evolving. If we lead a life of growth, it's pretty exciting. People get up with something inspiring to do each day. They say, *"I have something to accomplish, I'm important and I'm needed."* This is huge for a person's mental and physical health.

Without *purpose*, our minds can become focused on the negative, worried, empty inside and mentally distressed. These are the seeds of self-doubt and fear.

It is well known that an idle mind is the devil's workshop. Without focus, people often become dissatisfied and think of one problem after the other. The value of *staying on purpose* is needed to remain focused on what is possible and important.

How Courageous Leaders Unlock the Power of Collective Intelligence

When leaders believe they need to have all the answers, they often unintentionally cause others to feel diminished. Enhancing others by respecting other's thinking and unlocking the power of collective intelligence plays an enormous role in continually leading people, teams, organizations and communities to the next levels of desired Peak Performance. How do *Courageous Leaders* unlock the power of collective intelligence?

Let's picture Manager A entering a room. Manager A is smart, and they know they're smart, so they sound smart. They always have the answers, and they have a number of things to tell people, including their team members.

When this occurs, people stay quiet and hesitate to participate because Manager A has the answers. Team members know how smart Manager A is, so they hesitate to answer.

Instead of working together as a team to collaborate, plan and solve a problem, it's one person (Manager A, who is legitimately smart) coming up with the answers. What happens, usually unintentionally, is that others are diminished. The collective thoughts of others and the collective intelligence of the team is missed. Manager A walks in the room smart, acts smart and walks out of the room smart.

Now, let's picture Manager B entering a room. Manager B is also smart and capable. The objective of the meeting is explained, the direction of the team and updates on known parameters (budget, policies, available resources) are provided. Manager B works with the team to create a shared *vision* of the work and how the work is to be done.

Next, Manager B engages with the team, discussing the work objective from different angles and participating but not dominating the discussion. In fact, Manager B speaks about 20% of the time and team members speak about 80%. (Manager A speaks about 80% of the time.)

Manager A limits the group by having all the answers and acting smart, often thinking that's what is expected. Manager A (again, usually unintentionally) diminishes people, including team members.

What we see unfold is that Manager B is actually *Leader B*. Leader B intentionally invites everyone to be smart. Leader B asks important questions and facilitates team dialogue, possibilities as solutions emerge and innovative, quantitative results are discovered and delivered. Leader B invites and encourages the collective intelligence of the group. Leader B enhances people, including team members.

The intelligence of the group being led by Leader B will usually exceed Manager A, even if Manager A is smarter. When those being led are noticed, recognized and rewarded, they are most likely to become self-motivated and more engaged in their work. Remember, current research reveals only 30% of the people report they are engaged in their work[12]. Leader B can turn this percentage on its head and transform the percent of people engaged in being productive in their work.

Leaders are people who evolve beyond being stuck in their own heads and impressed by themselves. If we stay stuck in our own small bodies, we will never become bigger than ourselves.

We have to get outside ourselves (me, myself and I) to become bigger. People are not awarded for the good deeds they do for themselves. Leaders are recognized and rewarded for the good they do for others.

Take Action:

Utilizing collective intelligence to make a decision is the first step. Executing once a decision is made is where leadership makes the difference between ideas and results.

We often say, *"You haven't really led anything until you get a result."*

Below are three actions to consider when thinking about a leader's **decision-making execution** ability:

1. Ask, why bother?

What is the decision we're considering really about? If we ask, *"Why bother?"* and we can't answer that question in a very robust way, it may be a decision not worth spending a lot of time on. So, what is the *objective* and what is the *vision*?

2. Ask, why should I care?

If we ask, *"Why should I care?"* we can better understand if the decision is important enough to successfully execute. People need to understand *why* it is important and *why* they should care. Leaders are always working with team members to make sure they understand the *why* of the decision: *why* it's worthwhile for them to carry it out, what are some personal benefits, and what are the benefits to the organization and customers moving forward?

3. Take small deliberate steps.

Sometimes, improving little things can add up to make a huge difference. Often, with decision-making execution, people try to do it all at once. The real art and the real dance of this is in taking a step. Take a little step; improve something and then improve something else. Then take another step; improve something else, and be very persistent about doing this over and over as a way of being. A high percentage of people get distracted and give up along the way.

These are three actions to successfully execute decisions in a controlled and deliberate way to deliver results that are sustainable.

Changes need to be all about improving. So, don't be a *change-agent;* instead be an *"improvement-agent"* who creates a culture of constant improvement. Now, that is much more inspiring and motivating!

How Courageous Leaders Have Wisdom to Invest in Personal and Professional Development

An article was published by Gallup at the beginning of 2020 describing their findings for why some organizations have a much higher percentage of employees who are engaged[12]. The article affirms other research and what we have believed for many years. How do *Courageous Leaders* create requiring environments for leadership development?

What they found is what we have believed and observed for many, many years. The difference in the highly engaged organizations is development, specifically in leaders creating high-development cultures.

Once an organization has invested in and committed to development of team members, it is up to the leaders in the organization to create and sustain an environment that unlocks the potential created by that development.

Employees engaged in the development process are expanding their awareness of self and of others, discovering hidden biases and limiting thought patterns, seeing the world through different lenses, discovering new ways of being and increasing critical thinking abilities. It is now the responsibility of their leader to create and maintain an environment where individuals will use what they learned to grow through development.

We all know the old adage, "if you don't use it you lose it," and this thought really applies to these new learnings. Research shows that if new learning isn't applied within the first three days, the percentage drops significantly in terms of retention of new information. After a week, it drops dramatically again, and after a month, it's almost as if they haven't engaged in the development at all. After three months, the research shows the learning is essentially eradicated. The lesson here is it is all about application through practice, practice, practice.

Here are the kinds of environments that employees in organizations return to, all created by their leader:

1. They may come back to a **preventing environment**. It may sound like, *"Welcome back. I'm sure you are hearing about theories and different ways of being in your development. However, we won't be applying it here because we are already best in class with our performance."* This again can either come from what leaders say or from how they act.

2. People may come back to a **discouraging environment**. It may sound like, *"Hope you are having a good development experience. You know how we do things here, and we already do things extremely well."* Either by the leader verbalizing this or acting in a way that demonstrates this, the learnings are discouraged.

3. Employees may come back to a **neutral environment**. This sounds like, *"Hi, it's great to have you back. Hope you are having a good development experience."* This is very neutral

language and neither encourages nor discourages the application of their development.

4. We can could go the other way on the continuum to an **encouraging environment**. This may sound like, *"Hi, I'd love to hear what you are discovering and learning and how you think you can apply it!"* Their leader is very interested in what they are learning and encourages them to apply it in their work.

5. Going further on the continuum is a **requiring environment**. This is what leaders really want to have created and sustained. If people are going to apply what they've learned, they need to come back to a very robust discussion about what they learned. This may sound like,

    a. *"How will you apply what you are discovering and learning in your development?"*

    b. *"How will it make your team better?"*

    c. *"How will it help make your life better?"*

    d. *"How will it help make our organization better and the products and services to customers even better?"*

In a requiring environment, learning and discoveries are incorporated into work real-time and improve work performance.

Consistently integrating these new ways of being and better ways of working will determine the engagement of the people working in organizations, ultimately leading to the best performance for the organization. The most important thing is, people in

131

organizations will have a better work experience and hopefully go home to their families feeling more fulfilled and having better conversations with those around them.

The societal impact of this result is what inspires us to do the work we do every day. Research continues to confirm what we've believed for years:

When organizations truly care enough about the people they have been given the privilege to have working in them, providing the opportunity for development is a win for everyone involved. Organizations perform at their maximum potential, with leaders investing in and providing fulfilling work for the team members working in them, so they can deliver the best services and products for the people in their communities.

The opportunity is for leaders is to take team members where they would not go without them. Everyone is standing on the shoulders of their own current performance, going to the future, excited about delivering even better performance and results.

High-performance people, teams, organizations and communities are born from on-going development. There is no magical shortcut. High performance comes from dedicated, consistent leadership; it is hard won and not for the faint-hearted.

Chapter 7

Courageous Leaders Create Inspiring, Motivating Environments

Always take the next right step, and then the next.

How Courageous Leaders Create and Sustain Inspiring, Motivating Cultures and Families

Self-motivation and true self-accountability come from understanding what motivates others and articulating the organization's *mission, vision* and *strategy* in the language of team members. These attributes will be a huge factor in determining the success or failure of the organization's *goals* and *initiatives*. How do *Courageous Leaders* create and sustain inspiring, motivating cultures and families?

Sustained inspiration doesn't come from motivational speeches and feel-good initiatives. It comes from people finding ways to align the *purpose* of the work they do with their *personal purpose* for being on earth, including their natural interests, talents and capabilities. When team members understand how their work not only helps the organization deliver on its *mission* and *vision*, but also on their own personal *mission* and *vision*, a motivating and empowering environment is created and self-alignment is achieved.

We believe that when a person's personal *mission* is aligned with their organization's *mission*, the most powerful energy for improving the world is created.

To understand what motivates those on our teams takes curiosity, time and constant work. To build and nurture these relationships, teams cannot be so large (ideally 8-12 people per team) or they will likely have difficulty having enough airtime and space to fully contribute. When team size is less than five, there may not be enough diversity of views and opinions to challenge one another for innovation which we believe is the lifeblood of any organization. More than 12 can function more like a committee than a team. Functioning like a committee means some voices are dominant and others are crowded out with little airtime and dissipating energy.

It has been said that, to lead the many, we must lead the few. We often cite the example of Jesus, not as a religious figure, but as a leader who exemplifies leading the many by leading the few. By working with a dozen disciples, he reached the many.

Take Action:

Some questions to ask yourself:

- Are you multilingual, understanding the different languages (thought patterns) of those on your team?

- Does your language invite/require different perspectives and points of view?

- Does your language help relate team member's comments to one another?

- Does your language recognize and reinforce the value of divergent thinking?

- Does your language give credit to the ideas and solutions offered?

- Do team members think, feel and realize from their collective intelligence that they are smart and capable, so they want to and do participate?

Lifting those on our teams by developing, coaching and encouraging them, while providing available resources and removing barriers will empower them to lift the few on their teams and so on, eventually lifting and empowering all the people in the organization from one Peak Performance to the next.

We often discuss research that repeatedly shows the top two attributes team members say they desire in a leader:

1. **The leader is positive.**

2. **The leader creates a motivating, inspiring work environment.**

How can leaders create positive, motivating work environments? We know that energy is contagious. We always think about it as human glue.

Is the leader...

- Exuding human-glue relationships and positivity?

- Excited about the shared *vision* they created with their organization?

- In love with the organization's **mission** and **vision**?

- Excited about the organization's **winning proposition** (promise to the customers they serve)?

- Committed to by living into the organization's **values**, not just espousing them?

The leaders described above are absolutely positive because they are serving the **mission** of their organization or company. They want all the team members to serve the **mission**. It's all about the **mission** while pursuing the **vision**.

Leaders come and go, and they will over time. But if the consistent message is, *"We are all here to serve the mission!"* (and it's a really good one), then the environment will be an exciting and worthy place where they deliver products and services. We can hardly talk about that without getting quite excited!

Every action is **strategic**:

- Living according to shared **values**.

- Pursuing a shared **mission** every day.

- Delivering on a shared **winning proposition** as the promise to customers or clients.

- Pursuing a shared *vision*, where we want to be in the next 3 to 5 years.

That's really exciting because we all want to feel accomplished and successful. We can all make a good day, week, month, year and life!

Next, we begin asking questions about what we have to accomplish. What are our key *objectives* to get to the *vision*? What needs to be accomplished in the following *strategic perspectives*:

- *Financial stability* and *community impacts*.

- *Customer* or *client* services and products.

- Friendly, lean, effective and efficient *work processes*.

- *Diversity, equity and inclusion* in a *culture* that is inspiring and invigoratingly healthy.

When leaders are really focused on what's important (a few things and not everything), they begin to let go of what is really not very important. Work is prioritized and not just a pile that strains teams. A "stretch" is far different from a "strain."

Leaders help employees know exactly what's important. Everyone is linked and aligned. Everyone understands that saying no to a number of things enables them to say yes to where they want to go, how they're going to be with each other getting there, and what they will be delivering to their customers and clients.

With this kind of *mission-driven*, *vision-pulled*, *values-based* culture and an inspiring *winning proposition*, *Courageous Leaders* have the opportunity to create a motivating, inspiring environment that will really excite team members.

When people make a mistake, they understand it's just a learning opportunity. Shared *values* lived daily, help guide us in our decision making and gets us back on track if we slip up. If someone falls off the truck one day they know how to get right back on with the advantage of their learnings. When team members are doing new work for the first time or taking smart risks, there are always important learnings. In fact, life is one big experiment. When we do something that does not work, we learn to do it a better way.

People know what it takes to do well in this environment. There is synergy between the leader and the employees. It's just fantastic. That's the job of the positive leader.

There are so many choices in the world today. The positive leader says,

Let's get laser focused on the difference we can make with our employees to serve them better so they can serve our customers even better.

We believe we can get choice-laden. It's the job of the leader to not let that happen but to have the focus and excitement about where we are going and the things we must do to get there. Being clear and courageous does not leave team members guessing if they are doing the right thing. It is why real-time feedback, coaching and reinforcement requires intentional-attention from leaders.

We often talk with groups about *time mind travel*. Most of the time, we are either worrying about something that may happen in the future or ruminating about something that happened in the past. Even when we are physically present, our minds are usually traveling to some other place in time!

It's important for a leader to be **vision-pulled**. Setting a **vision** for the future is a key part of being a leader. But how does a leader, once that **vision** is set, stay in the present moment and not live in the future?

It is also important for a leader to learn from and extrapolate lessons from past experiences, both good and bad. So, how does a leader take lessons from the past and not dwell in the past?

When we focus on the future so much that it creates anxiety, it can take us out of the present. The same thing is true if we're focusing too much on the past. We may be associating guilt, regret or other negative feelings to a past event that can pull us out of the present.

The question for the leader is:

> **How can we stay in the present while bringing lessons learned from the past and be inspired by a compelling *vision* instead of feeling frustration from the past or anxiety about what might happen in the future?**

Take Action:

Three key actions that a leader can take are:

1. Remembering past events, negative and positive, and how they shaped the person that leader is today. That way the leader can bring the lessons from the past that helped develop their strength forward without dragging the baggage along with them into the present.

2. By setting a clear and inspiring *vision*, the leader can be pulled toward the *vision*, inspired and motivated by it, versus being stressed or anxious about an unknown future. The focus can be on the present moment and, what is that next step to work towards the *vision* and then the next, and the next…?

3. Be aware of the running inner-narrative in our minds. We are telling ourselves an ongoing story of what happened in the past and what may happen in the future. If the leader is feeling anxious, guilty, or whatever that feeling is at a particular moment, it is good to be aware of the story they are telling themselves. That story determines the quality of our lives and how successful we will be. A helpful question is, *"Am I safe and okay right now?"*

Science tells us it is impossible for our minds to be present 100% of the time. The three actions above can help leaders have more awareness of when they are not present and help them be present more often when it is most important. As author Eckhart Tolle says, *"The moment you are aware that you are not present, you are present."*

Leaders are always on stage. From the moment a leader enters a room, people are constantly watching and interpreting their body language, actions and possible mood. Truly being present when we are present requires moment-to-moment lifelong work and mastery.

It is life-changing when we don't easily believe all the stories we tell ourselves. Instead, just watch our stories go by like a movie while we sit back and not become the movie… just watch life unfold of which we have little control. This is the way of the calm, cool and collected person.

Overcoming fear and self-doubt to stop second-guessing ourselves is the greatest adventure of our minds. This is because fear hides in shame, resentment, anger, worry, depression, superiority, inferiority and many other hidden ways of our being.

What a waste of our precious days on this Earth. Taking our power back is crucial not just to existing but also to living! Creating our life where we are not living in fear and self-doubt is our biggest gift to ourselves and others. We become self-empowered to not waste our life. How can we not?

How Courageous Leaders Develop Cultures of 'Self-Accountability'

Another topic that comes up over and over again in our groups and in coaching is accountability. How do **Courageous Leaders** develop cultures of *self-accountability*?

It seems accountability is really quite elusive. When we talk with our clients about what their role as a leader is, we start with:

1. Setting very, very clear expectations (***goals, targets*** and ***timelines***) and being consistent about those standards.

2. Asking team members to give examples of what accomplishing those expectations looks like (actions and behaviors).

3. Asking team members if they understand why the expectations are important to successful performance.

When people have clear expectations for their deliverables (behaviors, products and services) and how they are going to do them, they now have the *what* and the *how*. Through these discussions, team members have the opportunity to be self-accountable to deliver on the clear expectations the leader has set. Self-accountability is the only true accountability, and it is the way people can become very proud of themselves and their accomplishments in life.

Only when there's accountability to expectations will people be responsible in their work. Team members have the opportunity for self-accountability, but we cannot hold others accountable. We hear this language all the time. We can hold others to compliance. This is very different than having an engaged workforce.

Year after year, Gallup Polls continue to show only about 30% of the people in the USA are engaged in their work. We believe that understanding the difference between developing self-accountability and holding people to compliance plays a major role in these dismal numbers.

How team members think about expectations and accountability leads them to the actions they can take to accomplish the results. Teams also determine if those are the results they want to achieve.

- Are they in line with the *mission*?

- Are they in line with their leader's expectations?

- Are they in line with their leader's intent for the work being done?

So, we could say just the reverse, right? Without accountability, there is no responsibility. Without responsibility, people don't think clearly about what needs to be done. When they don't take the actions, they don't get the results.

Clear expectations from the leader and self-accountability from the team-members to those expectations is where the magic is.

It seems that one thing that really helps with leaders we work with is getting to the desired specific actions and behaviors. What do the specific actions and behaviors look like and how will we work together to accomplish our *goals*?

When team members can envision how they will meet the expectations, we get to the actual behaviors (how people are going to do their work, how they're going to interact with others, how they're going to need to be).

Without clear expectations, consistency and team members understanding how they will meet those expectations, accountability is just a nice word that gets thrown around. Yes, everybody agrees that motherhood, apple pie and accountability are all wonderful. So, the real work is to live into self-accountability.

Leaders who provide clarity are kind, giving team members the opportunity to succeed again and again. Without clarity, as the "Father of Quality," Dr. Deming, used to say, *"We're off to the Milky Way."* It's pretty milky!

We have a lot of fun working together and working with our clients. We take our work very seriously and we share many laughs in the process! The best leaders use humor to create positive environments.

"Humor is a real secret tool of a highly effective leader." This doesn't mean telling jokes but just being humorous about whatever is being worked on at the time and leveraging our natural humor. We are all humorous in some way.

Some ways humor enhances the work environment are:

1. It Creates a Positive Work Environment

As we mentioned, the most important two characteristics that people say they desire in a leader are the following:

- The leader has a positive attitude.

- The leader creates an inspiring, motivating work environment.

An integral part of a positive work environment is that people have some fun and enjoy working together. It's good for people to laugh. Humor has a lot to do with creating a positive work environment.

We know that one of the two key responsibilities of a leader is to establish a positive, motivating culture. Humor is part of this positive culture where if team members so choose, will be self-motivated. Just bringing out the natural levity of people.

2. It Creates Balance

Another great advantage of appropriate humor in the workplace is that it's a nice balance so things don't get overly serious when hard work is being done. Balance is always such an important word. It's an important concept in the workplace. Humor is a major factor for balance.

3. It is Relational Glue

When appropriate humor is being leveraged as a part of the environment, it helps to build strong relationships.

People do more, and they do better when they really like the person they work for and when they can relate to them as a human being. Humor is part of being human.

We think of humor as an element of glue in relationships. We all have a certain degree of humor in us—a way of just being funny, where we can enjoy life in a very positive and constructive way. It builds wonderful relationships and helps to create team spirit, effectiveness and efficiency.

We know that a smile is the shortest distance between any two people. Humor helps create an uplifting and high performing culture. Appropriate humor is part of the environment and is actually a very big deal.

When we ask people to think of the best leaders they've encountered in their careers, the ones they really connected with always seemed to have a way of making them smile or laugh or bring some fun and humor into the workplace.

Leaders can create an environment where the work is enjoyable, it's warm and humor is a part of doing very important and hard work.

A major attribute of successful leaders is that they are relentlessly proactive in their adaptability and predictable in their *purpose* and behaviors. Adaptive leaders never think any two days will be the same with customer and employee needs. There is more than enough evidence that needs are progressive.

Too many leaders lose their way (and take their companies with them) by straying from worthy *missions, visions* and *values*... and at the same time, not reading, analyzing, actualizing and flexing to constantly changing customer needs and economic conditions.

An important question is, how can leaders be highly adaptable and rigorously predictable?

Take Action:

First, the greater ability leaders have to notice the needs, problems and opportunities that are constantly around them, the more agile they are in the following:

1. Creating clear direction.

2. Developing and coaching employees to become more independent in solving problems and providing the best solutions to customers.

3. Delegating work to provide growth options for team members instead of turning people into "ducks" lined up at the door to be fed every answer and to get approval for every decision they make.

4. Staffing projects with talented and creative team members where their leadership can flourish.

5. Seeing and leveraging the positive in difficult situations. Pain births growth. Letting pain exist while relaxing and letting it flow through and out of us is constructive human growth. We grow our strength when we feel the pains of life and stay patient as they pass through us.

6. We move fast enough, but not so fast as to churn ourselves and others. We go beyond excellence to the next level of Peak Performance.

Second, leaders need to be highly predictable in serving the worthy *mission* of their company. All business practices and dealings are aligned with deserving *missions*, *visions*, *values* and benefits to customers.

Corners are not cut, and integrity is not compromised. Leaders' decisions and behaviors come from a place of consciously and predictably pulling themselves to their higher selves. Employees, led by such leaders, are proactively living the *values* and serving the organization's *mission* while pursuing the evolving *vision*.

When the true compass for all work is aligned with the *why* of *strategy* (*mission, vision, values* and benefits to customers), the following is true:

1. Individuals and teams will be collaborative, results-oriented and high-performing.

2. Team members are proud to be working and feel they're working for one of the best organizations.

3. Employee ownership, self-accountability, innovation and productivity reach surprising heights of Peak Performance.

Take Action:

Some actions to consider:

- Actively seek and listen for challenges and problems to learn what still needs to be solved in the future.

- Be *strategic* in learning what, how much and how fast to improve in the immediate future and in the long-term.

- Enroll team members in the *why* of the next improvements and in how it will benefit them and their customers.

- Make conscious decisions to be and to stay in alignment with the worthy ***purpose*** and ***values*** of the organization.

- Be the positive leader everyone desires, not only demonstrating predictable, resilient behaviors in the good times, but also in times of failure and setbacks.

Through adaptable and predictable behavior, team members and leaders are stoic in mental and emotional grit and resilience, reliably delivering Peak Performance Results. People and teams live and lead with courage.

How Courageous Leaders Understand Trust as An Operating System™

Everyone talks about trust, but what does that really mean? We think about **Trust as An Operating System™** and we've created a simple equation for our conversations with leaders. How do *Courageous Leaders* use **trust as an operating system?**

The equation is:

$$\text{Tos} = \frac{C + C + C + C}{E}$$

On one side of the equation is **TOS: Trust as An Operating System™**.

The numerator in the equation are the four Cs of trust. The four Cs represent what years of the best research (very much aligned with what we experience in our work with leaders) indicate as the key factors that build trust.

The four Cs of trust:

153

1. **Competence:** Is the person competent to accomplish what needs to get done? Do I trust that the person has the experience and know-how to deliver on the desired results?

2. **Congruence:** Does the person say what they're going to do and then do it? Is there congruence between words and actions?

3. **Consistency:** We think of that as certainty or uncertainty. How consistent is the person we interact with? How certain or uncertain are we of how they will behave? Are they reliable?

4. **Character:** Do we view this person as honest and real, meaning appropriately vulnerable?

The denominator in the **Trust as An Operating System™** equation is **E: ego.**

In our equation, we think about ego as self-orientation. Do we have enough ego so that we're not a doormat, but not so much ego that we are egotistical?

If trust is going to be an operating system, we have to really use it as an operating system, making sure that self-orientation or the E in the equation, ego, is in balance with self and other orientation.

The four Cs may be present, but if the self-orientation (ego) is too high, it really wipes out the four C's in the numerator. In this case it is all about me, me, me and not much left for others. Why would anyone trust them?

Hiring new employees is one of the most important and costly things for businesses. People will obviously present their best selves in an interview. Asking the right questions and noticing answers using **Trust as An Operating System™** can help leaders better understand if they can trust a job candidate.

Below are some examples of how **Trust as An Operating System™** can be used in hiring conversations:

1. Hold the tension of knowing and not knowing. What we think we know about the self-orientation of a person we're hiring, for instance, must be balanced with a healthy respect for what we may not know. This way, we are very careful about the discussion we have with the person before we hire them or before we promote them. This tension can make us better in our decision making.

2. Slow down so we can think fast. Really try to see if the self-orientation of the ego is enough, too much, or just about right. Think about that rather than a more impulsive reaction. The four Cs may be wonderful, but how does self-orientation (ego) factor into the equation?

3. What are the questions at play? What questions have we really asked that go beyond just the technical part of one's work and get to the adaptive skill? Get to who they really are and what their self-orientation really is. Do they have their ego in tow? If a person is all about me, me, me and very little for you, why would anyone

155

trust that person regardless of strength in the four Cs?

A person may demonstrate the four Cs, but the question is, does their self-orientation cancel out the four Cs in the numerator?

If self-orientation is too high, a person may be *self-centered*. Again, everything is about me, me, me and very little is left over for you.

If a person's self-orientation is too low, they may be *self-less* to the point where fear and self-doubt causes them to believe they are not enough or incapable of successfully leading a team.

A person whose self-orientation is in balance, we say, is *other-centered*. They believe they can lead a team, an organization, a community, a movement, a cause, whatever it is they're leading to reach its **vision**, and they do it all in the service of others, not just for their own benefit or glory or self-aggrandizement.

Be sure to hire for good character, attitude and relational skills. Then consider technical content knowledge and skills which can be more easily taught.

Hiring is an incredibly expensive and time-consuming process, especially when someone doesn't work out. Trusting a person enough to bring them into a culture that a leader has so carefully created is a difficult task.

What we find so often, is that staffing is an activity in itself. Someone leaves and we're replacing that position with another person. That's staffing, and we do it over and over and over.

The question really becomes: staffing for what responsibilities and how does staffing enable the *strategy* of the organization to be supported and become a reality through people?

Take Action:

We think of it as being careful *not* to have the cart before the horse, and we hear it frequently. Instead of just filling a position, the questions really are:

- What is the *strategy* of the organization? What is the *strategic learning, planning and execution cycle*?

- What is the structure in the organization to enable the *strategy* to be successful?

- Within that structure, what are the positions?

- For each position, what are the responsibilities?

- Who is the best person or the best individuals (internally and externally) for the different positions based on those responsibilities?

By following this process in that order, we can get the best person into the best position. We don't want to hire people to take on a job. We want to hire people who see it as taking on the responsibilities of the position and making responsibilities very clear.

When this process is followed, people aren't just taking a job, they're having an opportunity to live who they are and leverage their strengths based on the agreed upon responsibilities. It's great for them because it becomes a self-projection of themselves beyond themselves through their daily work and chosen career.

Three things to think about based on our questions above:

1. Do we have a clear **strategy** of where we're going over the next three or four or five years?

2. What does the structure look like? Do we need a major part of our structure to be sales? Do we need a major part of our structure to be compliance to regulations? What is the needed structure?

3. What are the responsibilities for each position? We can then hire or promote people who are excited about the responsibilities and are a good match for them.

By maintaining *strategic leadership* through *strategic learning, planning, executing* and verifying at all times, we can avoid hiring just to replace or to fill openings. Now we have a chance

to get hiring right the first time, because it's linked and aligned all the way through the organization.

While carefully considering input from references and behavioral/motivational interviewing results, it is extremely important to study candidate resumes. By doing so, each candidate's education, experience, training, development and length of service (in each position) is revealed. Who is motivated for the short-term and who is motivated for the long-term, especially when the work is difficult and requires personal sacrifice?

Resumes revealing length of service in given positions is often significant information to be considered and should not be overlooked. When the going gets tough, resumes may reveal who is really courageous through pain and demonstrates true grit and resilience versus who just leaves and looks for the shiny penny and greener grass! Who lives and works courageously?

Chapter 8

Courageous Leaders Serve and Free People to Be Their Best Selves

Have others' best interest first and foremost, top of mind, and in our heart.

How Courageous Leaders are Flexible and Adaptable

The need to be adaptive and agile in a constantly changing world seems as relevant today as ever. When leaders are able to "bop and weave" with whatever life sends their way, they thrive. How do *Courageous Leaders* become more flexible and adaptable?

We often talk about change as the only constant. Adaptability is and will be the key to success. How adaptive people are determines their survival, and the same applies to teams and organizations.

Every team member chooses how she or he wishes to experience other team members and the work they do together. Can each person on the team, and then the team as a whole, be adaptable enough with each other to really deliver the best product or service to the customers?

We think about mental chemistry and how adaptability works in nature. Researchers studied parasites on roses. When roses dry up and die (after we cut them and bring them in the house, for instance), tiny parasites on the roses have an incredible metamorphosis. They sprout wings and leave the roses when they can't eat anymore from them. They fly to windows, doors or anywhere there's light to try to find and get the sources of food that will sustain them.

It is absolutely incredible to think about. A parasite living off a rose did not have wings, but it suddenly sprouts wings when the rose dies. This chemistry—the way that a parasite is able to *flex* themselves through metamorphosis to survive any condition they find themselves in—is pretty incredible.

So, what does it all mean for the different conditions and situations that teams and people are trying to solve? Three things come to mind:

1. How we think enables our wings to sprout through the solutions we create.

2. These solutions give our teams, organizations and companies innovative abilities and performance.

3. We can learn a lot from nature. In this case, parasites may be one of our best teachers.

Leaders can learn to be extremely agile by noticing what they can learn by the *tiniest* of life. Buddha is quoted as saying, *"I can learn from anything, even a rock."*

How Courageous Leaders Prioritize, Organize and Make Time

One of the most common themes we hear from nearly everyone we see is that no one has enough time. There never seems to be enough time in the day to get everything done. No one tells us, *"I have too much time and too many resources!"* One of the keys to being an intentional leader is understanding that no one has time, but leaders make time. How do **Courageous Leaders** make time and great days?

It is two words: ***prioritize*** and ***execute***. No one has enough time, yet we all have 24 hours in a day, so we have all the time there is. When you cut through all of it, we make time by prioritizing and executing.

Without prioritizing and executing we…

- Become overwhelmed.

- Get under the wave of too much to do and complete.

- Touch the same thing multiple times vs. working on it and completing it. (For projects that require coming back at a later date to work on, take it out and do the portion that is needed so it is complete for the time being.)

Take Action:

Some keys to prioritizing and executing:

- Align with *essence-symbols/images* (to be centered).

- Be intentional.

- Be focused.

- Stop falling distractions.

- Discipline our mind.

- Stop procrastinating.

In the long run, these are things that no one can do for us. We can never find time; we always make the time, or we don't make the time.

If we don't *make* the time, *make* an effective and efficient day, we will always be behind. We're not going to have enough time, we won't be focused, we won't be prioritizing, we won't be executing well, and we won't get the results that we need. This is what being a disciplined leader is all about.

To be a disciplined leader, we must...

- Have a sense of urgency.

- Have determination to win.

- Have resolve including the grit and resilience to do whatever needs to be done.

- Have an understanding of what I can and can't control. (Literally put what I can't control to the side.)

- Have an understanding of what's in front of me, what's the priority, what's the next step I can take and what's the next step after that.

- Humbly, take action, gain feedback and practice taking actions with the feedback again and again. This makes for fast learning cycles.

- Be *mission-pulled* and *vision-inspired*, delivering on specific performance *objectives*.

There's a lot of magic in this way of being. It's simple to say, but not simple to do. The magic is having a disciplined mind that is free from distractions to keep it simple: **Prioritize > Plan > Execute > Get Feedback > Practice.**

Continue with this feedback loop to gain discipline and mastery.

For example, a doctor finishes medical school and residency requirements, yet she spends a lifetime continuing to research and learn about her area of expertise. It needs to be the same for leaders. Ideally, we spend an equal amount of time studying our craft, studying leadership, and studying the art and science of human behavior.

Empowered people don't wait for great days, giving their power away. They make each day a great day and are self-empowered. *Constancy of purpose* fuels their path and creates *Courageous Leaders*.

How Courageous Leaders Connect with Others Through Best Intentions

The quality of the connections leaders make with the people they interact with impacts the amount of *influence* the leader has. This comes up often in our work with leaders. How do *Courageous Leaders* connect with others through best intentions?

As the bar is raised every year, more and more is expected from organizations, companies, and therefore, from people. The standards, requirements and expectations are rising and will continue rise.

What we find from leaders who are the most conscientious and caring is that, in conversations with those they lead, it's all about the following:

- What is the *purpose* of our work?

- How will we work together?

- What must be accomplished?

- What are the *timelines*?

- Do we have the needed resources?

- What are our first and next steps?

- Can we accomplish what we need to with shorter feedback cycle times?

Pausing for a moment to remember that as leaders we are talking with people and not a wall. Whether we like to think about it or not, actually we're all pretty fragile. We're human beings, with all our thoughts, feelings, actions and outcomes.

When leaders, consciously knowing that they're talking to a human being, make relational statements to drive out fear and self-doubt from those they lead, people are freed to do their best work.

These statements sound like:

- *"I know we can get through this together."*

- *"You are good at so many things, by improving this aspect of your work, you will make yourself even better."*

- *"It's good for your career and future."*

- *"This challenge is difficult for everyone, and you are going to be successful."*

- *"Wow, look at all the improvements and results you are delivering."*

- *"I really appreciate all the extra time and effort you're putting into this, and I hope that you are very pleased and proud of yourself."*

- *"It is easy to see how persistent you are being and how determined you are to make this work."*

169

These relational statements are an important part of developing the warmth of the leader. In fact, this is when leaders stay in the process, providing feedback to those they lead. However, the strong team members in the work process will determine the outcomes.

The bottom line is this:

Leaders stay in the process of coaching and reinforcing people and the work process will yield what it is capable of yielding.

Just as a well-formed golf swing delivers the ball to a much better location than an unskilled swing ever will. Leaders always coach people in the process—in what they are doing well and in how they can perform even better.

If it's just about what we have to do, how fast we have to do it, what the expectation is, and all of the bars we have to jump, we lose that connection. If we forget that we're actually talking to a person and we forget to observe this warmth, this human glue that holds us together, people start to feel like a machine. It becomes, *"How much blood can you give me today?"* In the long run, that approach doesn't in any way foster that connection between the leader and the person they're leading.

We must have this connection (this warmth and humanness) where people want to go in the direction and do what we need them to do. They don't just have to do it, but they want to do it because they know that we care about them and know we're investing in them and their growth potential.

Leaders understand there is nothing "soft" about this kind of leadership. Leaders believe in the full potential of every human being. They are willing to have investment conversations because they want the best for team members, their organization and their customers. Leaders who truly care about those they lead stand in the space of possibility for each person. They are sure to invest in them and not let them miss the opportunity to become their personal best.

As we discussed earlier, when people are asked who their favorite teacher was in school, they don't name the easy one. They name the tough teacher. We ask why it was the tough teacher. They tell us, *"Oh, with that teacher, I studied harder; I worked harder; that teacher helped me become more successful and an even better person."* This person felt the teacher invested in them.

That combination of expectations, warmth, investment and caring is something you can't put a price tag on. It makes the big difference for people self-actualizing, their work being optimized, and their success being optimized, and it changes the world for each person they lead!

A question we often get asked in many different ways has a common theme that plays out. It is depicted as follows:

"I'm in a meeting. I give accurate information. I think very carefully about the answers I give. I

know the answers I'm giving are good answers, yet, I have difficulty. It'll come back to me that I wasn't nice, was emotional or I was controlling. Somehow, I didn't connect with the group. Other executives that I was talking with tell me, I really am a subject matter expert in the information that I'm providing. Sometimes, I'll find out that I'm really viewed as needing help in terms of my leadership, and not yet ready for taking on more responsibility."

So, the question is, *"Why is it that I feel that I'm an outsider and that I don't connect, or, in the worst case, I am invisible when future leadership positions are considered?"*

Most of the leaders we work with are incredibly well studied, and think deliberately and intentionally about what they're doing and saying. This in fact, often results in the real issue. It isn't just the accuracy of the information we're putting out there or what we're saying. It's how we're saying it that may not get enough consideration in one's self-awareness.

If we put it out there in too much of an emotionally firm, determined way, it doesn't feel inclusive to others and/or that we are not well regulated and balanced in our views, meaning too opinionated. What we offer as a fact is really a point of conversation with others. When leaders are not conversational in their language, fear and angst are created.

Questions to consider:

- Is how I'm delivering this message conversational?

- Is how I'm delivering this message collaborative?

- Is how I'm delivering this message inviting collective intelligence from others?

- Is how I'm delivering this message helping others feel smart by including them?

- Are we consistently asking others how they feel about our message and what they think about the message we just put out?

- Are we consistently seeking out the meaning they are giving to our message and what their recommendations would be?

It is this inclusive way of speaking, not just an accurate way of speaking, that enables a leader to be smart but not the only smart one in the room. By making others smart and getting collective intelligence, people will feel included and not overpowered. They become interested and engaged. People are not just taking up room in a chair.

If a team of people feel overpowered by someone because of how smart or accurate their answers are, then it really does put a separation between that leader and those they are speaking to, regardless of how accurate the information is. The person could be dead right.

The real lesson is:

When anyone of us thinks we know everything with too many right answers, we sacrifice relationships with others who then feel less than and not recognized as smart. Our relationships may be in trouble and we don't even know it. Perhaps, we do not even have a clue to what we are generating.

The question is, does our presence result in others feeling smart, included in the conversation and in the solutions and outcomes from the conversation? People engage by doing.

The art and science of communication is not only the importance of what we say, but even more importantly how we say it to generate intended thoughts and feelings in others – our audience.

The better the leader, the more they invite, require and provide space for the voices of those they lead. By slowing down up front to gain diverse perspectives, leaders can then implement much faster because employees hear their voice and see themselves in the work and solutions. Slow down to think in order to go fast forming and implementing solutions.

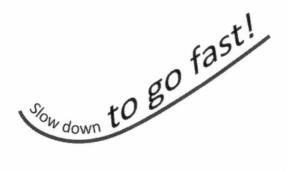

Slow down to get buy-in and to eradicate the root cause, and then implement solutions quickly.

Here, again, we are able to see the importance of a great marriage of the *what* and the *how*, and how frequently the *how* will eat the *what* for lunch!

Many decades ago, there was a wonderful field of research and study called transactional analysis and we use it to describe tone of voice with leaders.

As we mentioned earlier, about 38% of how we interpret communication is through the tone of voice of the speaker[13]. In his work with transactional analysis, Eric Berne describes three tones of voice – child, parent and adult – to describe how we communicate[14].

We think of the **adult voice** as the **leader-coach**. Part of coaching is developing the coachee's ability to use critical thinking skills to figure out their best solutions. In a coaching conversation, it is important to maintain Berne's adult voice.

Berne's **child voice** comes through as the *victim* when people tell a story. Often people will tell a story and will not see themselves in it except in the role as the victim of the story. The situation, or circumstances, are causing the person's discontent.

Berne's **parent voice** often comes through as the *hero* of the story. Often, if the person isn't the victim of their story, they are the hero of it. They fix what everyone else does wrong.

When we are being a leader-coach, we ask questions to help the coachee better understand the following:

1. Their role in the situation.

2. How they are being impacted by the situation (current reality).

3. How they want to be in the situation (desired reality).

4. Ideas that they come up with to take action and move from their current reality to their desired state, transforming her/himself.

The leader-coach listens for and reflects the meaning of what the coachee is saying.

The leader-coach is…

- Cool, calm and collected. It is not about them. The leader-coach is intentionally present for the coachee.

- Rational and objective.

- Emotionally regulated.

- Compassionate

They ensure coachees identify action steps to be strength-based in improvement.

Many people simply haven't had a chance to really develop their adult voice. The adult voice is really the critical thinking self—the ability, instead of being a victim or hero of the story, to use critical thinking skills (to use one's own power) to change whatever situation they're in, by transforming themselves.

Leaders we work with start to hear the victim story (or the child's voice) when interacting with others. They hear things such as, *"They keep doing this to me,"* or, *"The circumstances happened to me."* It's always about something happening to the person or being done to them.

The hero story (or the parent's voice) sounds like, *"Well, they came to me, and I told them to do this, this and this, and it solved it,"* or, *"They came to me, and they had all these problems, and I gave them direction, and they went and did it."*

The problem with the child's voice, of course, is that people are giving up their power (when they are the victim) and giving their power away to the situation. They are in need of a hero, someone in the parent role.

The problem with the parent's voice is, if we are always fixing problems for others and being the hero, then other people aren't developing their own critical thinking skills and taking constructive actions, so they remain in the victim or child/dependent role. We create a parade of ducks coming to us to be fed solutions to their problems.

It's important to move to adult-to-adult interactions and conversations because they are really good for everyone as critical thinking skills are strengthened and independence is fostered. Now, those we lead are well on the road to self-accountability, and leaders never again need to live the illusion that they can or need to hold others accountable.

People capable of learning how to be self-accountable for their own words and behaviors become great contributors.

We all need to develop powerful critical thinking skills in order to function as strength-based problem solvers. By reframing problems and challenges into opportunities to develop our critical thinking skills, we can transform fear and self-doubt into living and leading with courage. That is how to make a rewarding life!

Chapter 9

Courageous Leaders are Curious Lifelong Learners

Be mindful. Practice taking disciplined, right actions.

How Courageous Leaders Make It Their Business to Understand How People Tick

Our work with clients to help them become more *strategic* is most important for them as they take their organizations to the future. How do ***Courageous Leaders*** make it their business to understand how people tick?

Leaders work hard with their teams to be successful. If they haven't developed a *strategy*, there may be a lot of hard work, and there may be a lot of activity, but there might not be much progress.

Even if there is a *strategy*, it is often just pretty wallpaper or a big, thick notebook that sits on a bookshelf and collects dust.

Each person on the team may have a slightly different view of what the outcomes need to be, what was said, what they remember or what they don't remember. One team member may think, *"I thought we were going in this direction and everything was really clear."* Another team member may think, *"This is not very clear at all. I'm not sure where we're going."*

Confusion happens more often than not.

Take Action:

Leaders can do more of the following to be more *strategic* in their team leadership:

181

1. Create a shared *strategic mission* and *vision*.

   - Clarify what is our *why purpose,* which is *mission*?

   - Determine what *vision* to pursue in creating the desired future?

   They are very directional and gives the team a clear next destination to work toward within a certain timeframe.

2. Identify the big *objectives* (accomplishments), *goals* we must achieve, *measures* and *timeframes* for these desired results.

3. Determine when to accomplish each *objective* based on established delivery *targets*.

4. Plan how progress will be made.

   - What improvements are needed?

   - What are the *projects*?

   - Who will do what? By when?

   - What are the project deliverables?

When we get specific and clear, we not only have work sessions and work hard, but also are laser-focused. Leaders can now be *strategic* instead of everyone doing various versions of their best. The leader aligns everyone to create a clearly delineated future, and they minimize waste, rework and conflict caused by lack of clarity. *Strategic leadership* can be far more productive and rewarding for team members and company success.

This process creates the unifying structure that provides coordination and clarity to people and their work.

This comes up often when leaders work with us in development and then struggle to find time to implement what they've learned.

Researching and learning on their own is also something leaders tell us is a struggle. Often, leaders will have technical expertise or general expertise about leading people that got them to where they are today. At this point, the best leaders realize the following:

"I am also the leader of people and had better feed my brain very fast getting the development about what it means to be a leader: the manager part, the leader part, on to the leader-manager, and eventually, how do I become the leader-coach, the leader-teacher and so on up the leader's capability curve."

It really takes study and development in the area of leadership to be a *Courageous Leader*. A brain surgeon puts in a lot of time to continue to grow as a brain surgeon. How much time leaders make to read, study and develop as a leader is an important question for all leaders to think deeply about.

The law of attraction determines so much about our lives. Throughout history, philosophers and deep thinkers have come to the same conclusion: we literally become what we think about. The predominant thoughts in our minds will attract the things we think about into our lives, literally making us into who we are.

Take Action:

For *Courageous Leaders*, understanding the law of attraction is critical. To better understand the law of attraction, ask:

1. **What am I currently attracting into my life?**

   Many things will be positive, and many things won't be as positive. Awareness of our thoughts and what they attract into our lives is key to creating the life we desire.

2. **What is it that I really want in my life?**

   By changing our thoughts, we change what we are attracting into our life.

3. **How can I consistently refocus my thoughts on my desired self?**

   Imagine our future self as who and what we want it to be. What is our future self trying to accomplish? What impact is our future self leaving on earth?

By retraining our mind to focus on our desired future self, we will attract into our lives the things we need in order to become that future self. Conversely, if we focus on negative aspects of life, we will instead attract those things.

Imagination creates reality. It is vital for leaders to have that kind of possibility creation. Actually, the past is over, and today is the first day of our lives. The quality of our future will always be about what we make it from this day forward, no more and no less.

We are constantly creating our personal atmosphere which is the weather we bring to ourselves and determines how others will experience us. If we mentally and emotionally bring bad weather (which will first impact us and then others), we will negatively impact them. When others reflect our weather back to us, we become angry with them, and our own weather becomes worse. When those who have been impacted by our weather absorb and then spread our weather onto others, we've now begun multiplying our contagious, negative energy, and we may never know how far it will spread.

On the other hand, if we bring great weather, we will positively impact our own selves and then others. Again, this positive energy may spread far beyond what we will ever know. It may circle the world, positively impacting countless other beings.

Life is way too short to destroy our wellbeing and negatively impact the wellbeing of others. We can lead from where we stand to be an igniting force for all.

How Courageous Leaders Build Their Reputation Through Uncompromisable Character

Many leaders ask us about the difference between a company's reputation and its character, and they wonder which is real. How do *Courageous Leaders* build their reputation through uncompromisable character?

Both character and reputation can be real. Reputation that results from character is real. We also believe that reputation can be bought and faked. We find many organizations begin as a character-based organization. Over time, as they build character, they gain the reputation that comes from the character.

The problem we see is when organizations begin to focus on their reputation and lose sight of the character that originally built their good reputation. As soon as the organization becomes reputation-focused, there is a chance that they'll lose that character that initially existed as the foundational building blocks.

We hear of many ways organizations are trying to protect their reputation. When employees leave, organizations may not conduct exit interviews. Also, to protect their reputation and to inflate retention numbers, they may retain people who are not a good fit for the organization and not performed for years.

When companies flip their focus to an outside perception of what the company is versus what they truly are, exit interviews aren't conducted, or employees aren't let go that should be. This is when the character behind the reputation begins to erode.

Employees tell the real story to each other, friends and family, and it is very different from what the public sees and believes. The public tells one story while employees know (and sometimes tell) the real story.

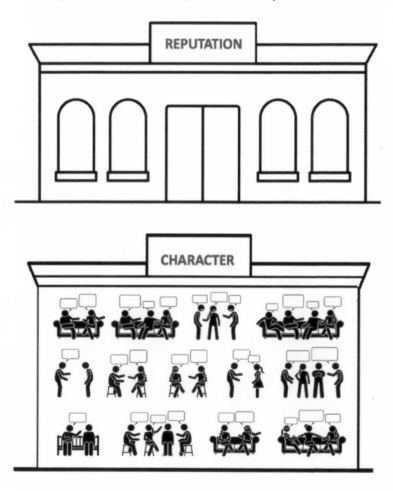

We work with our clients in many different areas of their business. We help them have an even higher performing organization that grows from peak to peak in terms of performance. We work to help organizations build character through making decisions, behaving and living in alignment with *mission, vision, values,* and lean operational best practices, *not* posting them on walls and then acting contrary to what they say.

Words mean nothing without aligned actions. In fact, we feel that it is better to not have *values* at all rather than hanging them on a wall and then not living them. We believe in diverse and inclusive *customer-pulled, employee-first* cultures of continuous, expansive improvement. It is developed and created from within. Character cannot be bought because employees know the truth.

Organizations that truly want to have a better understanding of what employees really think about their culture often make regular use of pulse surveys. Pulse surveys can get behind the real internal perception of character in an organization.

The survey must be specific to what is most important to know, and it must ask questions that reveal what people actually think versus what management wants to hear. As the culture evolves the organization has a wonderful opportunity to have an *intentional-attention culture* that pays laser-focused attention not only to what the outside thinks, but more importantly, what employees really think and how well aligned are the two perspectives.

Reputation is extremely important to attract the best employees and the best customers. When built from character, the story employees tell about the organization will align with the stories the public tells.

That's critically important, because when employees go home to their families, would they advise their best friend or relative to join the company? Do we have a match between reputation and what employees are saying?

We also find a stark difference between what employees say to their manager, owner of the company or senior leadership team members and what they say to their families and other employees.

That's the real story. What do people say when senior team members aren't looking? What they do and say when others aren't looking is the true character of the organization.

In the long run, we get real productivity when people use their discretionary time thinking of their work and how they can improve it.

Leadership is the *game changer* and has as much *'presence'* when leadership behaviors are missing. Then we experience the sad difference between lack of leadership and *Courageous Leadership*. We can find examples of both in organizations big and small, in government and world leaders. Lack of leadership can be devastating in individual lives and on a societal scale.

For each of us, what is our positive direct impact and circle of *influence*?

What is our intention?

How Courageous Leaders use Huddles to Build Family and Work Team Success

We are often asked if there is a more effective and efficient way for team members to regularly calibrate for better quality and timely outcomes without getting involved in long conversations that take up everyone's time. How do *Courageous Leaders* use huddles to build family and work team success?

Huddles are a simple and effective forum where employees are taught to participate in continuous improvement. Small groups of employees who do similar work, regularly meet (at least weekly) for 30-40 minutes in a facilitated discussion led by the supervisor, or they rotate facilitation among themselves. This is an important part of the workday and is held on company time.

During huddles, the work of team members is to...

- Generate insights to prevent mistakes and near misses.

- Identify problems with how they do their work and any resulting issues with their products or services.

- Analyze the cause of problems and create best solutions.

Take Action:

To use huddles for continuous improvement:

1. Identify problems and potential problems.

2. Analyze the scope of the problem and causes.

3. Identify root causes.

4. Create solutions to eliminate root causes.

5. Implement the agreed upon solution.

6. Monitor the results and verify the improvements have been made.

7. Adjust and refine corrective actions as needed.

A few of the key problem-solving tools to use in Huddles include the following:

- Flow charts.

- Pareto charts (most results come from a few causes).

- Cause-and-effect diagrams.

Huddles are not a forum for discussing salary/benefits issues. Instead, they are the forum for employees to discuss service, product and process improvement.

Huddles are a crucial tool for leading teams to ever better Peak Performance Results. This is true employee engagement in decision making, improvements and innovation. Actually, the degree of employee engagement and productivity jumps to the top of the chart when Huddles are alive and well as a methodology for moving teams to increased success.

Now we are no longer just giving lip services to desiring employee engagement. Instead, team members are actually involved in the doing of producing better quality solutions, products and services and, ultimately making their work life better and much more meaningful.

We all learn the most by *noticing* and *doing*!

Some of the best leaders we've encountered have been excellent storytellers. People in organizations carry out all kinds of different work. The real question is, what is the human-interest stories behind the work story? Everything gets done through people, so what is that human-interest story that people will be interested in hearing and learning about?

When the leader is a wonderful storyteller, it brings to life the human-interest story behind all the products and services an organization provides. That is what really inspires and interests people.

Take Action:

Here are three areas where a leader can be a wonderful storyteller:

1. Telling a story about challenges in the business and what people have done that has made a difference, and how much that is appreciated.

2. Telling a story about how people have grown in their confidence and in their determination to make the products or services a success.

3. Telling a story about the human relationships and how people have helped each other accomplish their work.

When the day is done any form of business is an intricate web of relationships. When the leader can be that storyteller, it brings ideas to life. In the end, we are all humans who get inspired by good human-interest stories.

It is a big, teachable moment when team members hear and understand what is most important to their leader and their leader's moral compass is revealed. These realizations are best expressed through stories as they reveal our *values* in our personal and professional life.

As people in organizations are promoted, we often hear the question of how they can successfully move from being a peer to a leader of their peers. The transition can be awkward, or it can be very graceful, depending on how the leader views it.

Take Action:

There are three things that come to mind that can make the transition smoother:

1. **First, have a clear understanding that the job of everyone in the organization is to deliver on the organization's *mission* and work towards a shared *vision*.**

   Leaders must be very clear early on that nobody works for them—everyone works for the *mission* and towards the *vision*. Simply put, the job of the leader is to consistently ask themselves, for all the people who report to them, what is it that they need to best live the *mission* of the organization?

   - Do they need coaching?

   - Do they need training?

   - Do they need development?

   - Are there barriers in their way?

   - Are there resources that they need?

- What is it that is getting in the way?

- What could make things more efficient and effective?

2. **Second, make it a smoother transition from peer to leader by understanding accountability, specifically what true self-accountability is.**

We hear so much about people wanting to "hold others accountable," and it's kind of a buzz word and something people default to. I often wonder what the answer would be if we were to ask people, *"What does holding somebody accountable actually look like?"*

Self-accountability is when somebody understands and is working toward the *vision* of the organization through *objectives, initiatives, projects* or *activities*.

The leader's job is, through coaching, to ask the right elegant questions of those they lead to help them develop self-accountability. If, through this coaching, each person on a team is consistently telling the leader where they currently are, where they need to be and what actions they are taking to best live the ***mission*** and work toward the organization's ***vision***, self-accountability becomes part of the organization's culture. Without self-accountability, everyone is being held to compliance with positional authority and negative consequences. Compliance is *not* self-accountability and will not lead to engagement.

3. **Finally, consistently verify that the action items each team member is committed to are being achieved.**

   Verify that progress is being made. What isn't measured usually isn't accomplished. Verification begins with each person knowing what their roles and responsibilities are and having very clear expectations that are established within those roles and responsibilities. Each person has to have a way to verify that they are accomplishing whatever it is they're responsible to deliver. Then each person can tell the entire story of their work: why, how and what they do to be successful by when. Then each person can tell the entire story of their work: why, how and what they do to be successful by when.

The transition from peer to leader hopefully can be more graceful by embodying these three practices.

Chapter 10

Courageous Leaders' Wounds Provide Their Leadership Wisdom

It is through adversity that we have the opportunity to grow, be courageous and gain wisdom through our life experience

.

How Courageous Leaders Leverage Mistakes and Failures as Powerful Learnings

We all face challenges and experience pain. Challenges in life and in our careers have the opportunity to be our best friends. How do *Courageous Leaders* view mistakes and failures as the beginnings of powerful learning?

Through challenges, we transform and become who we are today. We encourage leaders to welcome transformation, because that's the way they can avoid capping themselves and their organizations as well as having great work to pursue for the rest of their personal and professional lives.

We once asked a group of leaders we work with what current challenges they were facing, and they spent some time discussing many negative things that were out of their control. One of the leaders asked, *"Why ask a question that triggers a negative conversation?"* Our response was, *"Why do challenges have to be something negative?"*

Writer and philosopher Martin Buber spoke of, *"Living on the ridge of life."* He saw challenges as things we can *"fall in love with,"* because they help us grow and evolve our very being.

Take Action:

There are some very specific ways of being and actions we all can take to 'greet our challenges' and grow from them.

When faced with a challenge, the leader needs to be...

- Aware of what the challenge is.

- Focused and disciplined in dealing with that challenge. Get their head around it and determine how they are going to be and what they are going to do while facing this challenge.

- Patient with themselves. Have a timeframe that is reasonable. We can't always meet a challenge tomorrow. It often takes a lot of work, practice and patience.

- Know that these are the challenges now and there will be many, many more challenges in the future. These challenges are the way the leader will evolve and how those they lead will also grow.

- Stay humble and do the real work.

- Verify desired results from implementing their plan.

Challenges are really our next steps of development, and they are a key part of our personal and leadership transformation. Leaders grow through taking on challenges and transforming. As leaders grow, others in the organization are not bumping their head on "leader" ceilings.' Leaders are always moving up the performance curve and developing others to do the same.

What is awkward or hard today can be easy tomorrow. Adversity is how we develop our mental, emotional and physical grit, resilience and maturity for a life full of accomplishments.

Through challenges we transform. We encourage leaders to be very glad to transform, because that's the way they can avoid capping their organization and their life. They continuously move up, up, up the curve through overcoming challenges and transforming. This way, others in the organization are not bumping their head because their leaders have become blockers in the organization. The leader is always moving and developing others. Challenges are a key part of our personal and leadership transformation.

Nelson Mandela once said, *"I learned that courage was not the absence of fear, but the triumph over it."* - Nelson Mandela

Difficult times are when leaders are needed the most. The greater the challenge, the greater the need for leaders to step up. Anytime we face something we have not experienced before, fear and doubt may appear. Triumphing over these obstacles is how leaders develop and grow.

As Nelson Mandela's quote indicates, fear will always be there. It is what leaders think, say and do that will determine how they will lead through any challenge. This is when the work leaders have done on their own development is needed the most. This challenge is what leaders have been preparing for.

Take Action:

Below are three simple thoughts for leaders to ask themselves to find center when leading through any challenge:

1. Be still for a moment. It is ok to be afraid. Our fears are not special. Millions (or billions) of people have the exact same thoughts, worries and fears. Leaders understand we can choose how we will be, regardless of the situation. Ask, *"What is my essence? What is my best energy?"*

2. Think about, in vivid detail, one thing you are especially grateful for right now. Even in the toughest of times, there is so much to be grateful for. Gratitude is a great weapon against fear and self-doubt.

3. Imagine your future self. Who will you visit and appreciate first? What will you do differently? How will you be even better as a result of this difficulty?

Any time a leader feels fear, they know that this is when true grit, resilience and determination are being summoned. Finding the will to move forward, the will to overcome and the will to triumph is what leaders are called to do. Tough times call for tough leaders, and this is when we all grow the most, far more than in the easy times. Leaders *ignite* themselves and others by taking on what others think is impossible, gravitating to the steepest hills. It is where the most learning and growing will be discovered.

Why waste a second to know more and better so we can then be more and better for ourselves, family, work team members and community? We will not get one second back, because time is not a renewable resource.

How Courageous Leaders are Forever Students Who Value and Grow from Adversity

It has been said that adversity does not create character, it reveals it. During the greatest of challenges, as well as the daily trials and tribulations we all face, leaders are either stepping up and growing themselves and their teams or they are being pulled down by the circumstances. How do *Courageous Leaders* forever remain students who value and grow from adversity?

How we deal with adversity reveals who we are as leaders and whether or not we will be more powerful in our impact for the good of everyone.

Leaders become who they are (in many ways) through how they deal with adversity. Their response to the natural adversity and drama that is a part of daily life, or the extreme adversity in great challenges, helps develop and refine their leadership style and capability. Seeing adversity through this lens, leaders can begin to see challenges as friends.

By learning and growing, leaders are either used by the experience or they use the experience to further develop themselves and to develop others. The experience becomes an opportunity to magnify the best in themselves, defeat what limits them, and become stronger, more confident and better at serving leaders.

Along the humble journey of ever-striving to earn trust and *influence* others, leaders encounter unlikely friends. These friends are often presented as adversity, problems, unprincipled situations, and difficulties.

Of course, we do not wish for bad things to happen to anyone, but we know that life is made up of one challenge after the next. Making adversity our friend doesn't mean being friends with the circumstance or negative situation. It means discovering our best selves as we meet each adversary.

Take Action:

Some questions for leaders are:

1. When adversity presents itself, can we use the opportunity to grow ourselves and our teams through the adversarial situation?

2. Can we turn a negative situation into an opportunity to be even better as a leader, as a family member, as a human being?

3. Can we create something positive out of something negative? It is the true way to combat the negative forces in the world. Turn them upside down. Use them to change things for the better.

4. Can we stare down our fearful self and ask ourselves what that fear is telling us about ourselves - what is our work to grow and mature?

When leaders *make adversity their friend*, it is an introduction to themselves, because they can see their response to difficult situations and, who they have truly become. Our volition to enhanced being and performing is hard earned.

Learning who they have become is their next starting point to further build their strength and character to take on the next test of improved leadership. Every day, each of us as leaders in our own lives, *create the 'worthiness' of our leadership*. Leaders become who they are (in some ways) through everyday adversity and drama. The natural adversity and drama that is a part of many days can be viewed as the unexpected and true friends of leaders.

Along the way, leaders realize they are developing their character by not letting themselves be pulled down to the level of many circumstances, but instead, pulling themselves up to the level of the challenge that adversity and drama present.

When leaders evolve, it is their next starting point to further build their strength and character to take on the next test of improved leadership.

13th Century poet and philosopher Rumi said that, *"The wound is the place where the light gets in."*

It is true for big things and seemingly small things that happen in a day. During a group work session, a team member may make a cutting remark directed towards the group leader. Whether this comment was made to intentionally hurt the group leader or not, the damage has been done. The work session may continue and seemingly finishes in a good place. However, the group leader leaves feeling putdown, angry and embarrassed.

Days pass and feelings of resentment and dejection set in. How can this group leader best cope with what has occurred?

How we frame events in our lives, both uplifting and (maybe to a greater degree) painful, determine if we grow from our experiences or become victims.

- What lessons can this group leader take away from what occurred?

- How will he better handle a similar situation in the future?

- What did this group leader learn about another's level of maturity and self-awareness?

- What did the group leader learn about themselves?

- Do we grow through the discomfort of pain or do we run from pain? Pain can give birth to strength and growth.

If we live as life-long learners, all experiences become opportunities for growth. Our deepest wounds can become our greatest teachers. Our stronger future selves are born from learning and from the true grit, resilience, determination and persistence of ascending the new peak of our performance. To know what our future will be, we need to carefully consider our actions today because they create our future.

We live in the age of interruption and often hear from leaders how interruptions disrupt their daily workflow.

Interruptions and adversities are a part of life. They are a real and expected part of the journey. They are a part of the leader's work and the leader's responsibility to others. Adversities are our friends because they push us to be better.

In essence, this is the story we often hear from leaders we work with:

"We start the day with a plan and imagine how we're going to work the plan. Then this happened or that happened, and it wasn't what I expected during the day. Interruptions derail us from our plan, and we don't accomplish what we intended to start or complete."

As we work with our clients and reflect on what they thought their day was going to be like, they talk about the interruptions as if they are an appendage that flies in from the side somehow into the mainstream. We hear that these interruptions (or appendages) are really very much a part of their daily life.

And yet, as we discuss these interruptions further, leaders we work with realize they and their teams learn from these interruptions some of the most valuable lessons in their work and in their lives. The interruptions are extremely instructive. They learn this even though they don't like these interruptions. They don't like the *pain*, but they appreciate the lessons learned.

Why are interruptions so instructive and a part of the path—a part of life's journey?

These difficulties…

- Push us to excellence.

- Push us to be more innovative.

- Push us to find answers.

- Push us to be quick on our feet.

- Push us be flexible in the moment.

- Push us to be spontaneous.

- Push us to be innovative.

- Push us to be creative.

- Push us to be intuitive in the moment.

- Push us to listen, ask and be more present.

- Push us to be inclusive by valuing different thoughts, perspectives and ways of contributing.

- Push us to work smarter.

- Push us to do more and more.

- Push us to be more reasoned, patient and mature.

- Push us to not give up and to not give in to our fears and self-doubts.

Interruptions are really not interruptions at all. They give us some of the finest opportunities as leaders to lead and for teams to perform.

We recommend leaders differentiate between what's an interruption that detracts from the work and what's an interruption that actually adds to the experience, increasing learning and innovation?

Sometimes interruptions arise when people are not feeling empowered enough to see a situation and to come up with their best solution; instead, they feel the need to constantly ask their leaders for approval before making a decision. This kind of interruption means the leader must constantly tell, tell, tell. Team members haven't developed or aren't required to use their critical thinking skills. This is in contrast to leaders requiring team members to always bring their best thinking and offer their best solutions to their question before asking their leader.

Solutions first, then answers help team members realize what they already know and don't need to ask.

Some interruptions are caused by systems issues that often result in poor workflow, motivational issues and lack of self-accountability. These are the kind of interruptions we want to notice very carefully, take meaning from, and see what we can learn from them as we go along the path of leading people to do even more excellent work.

In this age of interruption, as we try to block interruptions from our life, we may be blocking out some of the greatest teachers of our life.

When we ask our clients what they think made them into the leader and the person they are today, they'll almost always talk about facing their fears, overcoming their lack of confidence and successfully dealing with difficulties that you would never want in your life.

For those who want to transform their difficulties into improvement opportunities and grow their grit and resilience, great personal growth and character is enhanced and further developed during adversity. Turn *struggle* and any *pain* upside down to be valued as the price of freedom.

In fact, people begin to realize that interruptions don't pull us away from our life's path, they are an integral part of our path. Interruptions are this thing called LIFE.

It is very rewarding when we experience those we work with becoming more accountable, less fearful and more courageous in their own growth and behaviors. They are *IGNITED*!

How Courageous Leaders Have the Tenacity to Strengthen Their Voice to Change the World

Many leaders tell us they have difficulty getting their voice in the room or they have trouble speaking in front of groups. For many, when it comes to a large audience, it's just unfathomable. They can't even imagine doing that. How do *Courageous Leaders* find the tenacity to strengthen their voice to change the world?

Each time it's studied, people's number one fear is public speaking. Number two is death. Almost everybody who gets up to speak in front of a crowd, or even in front of a small group, has butterflies. We work with many, many leaders on pushing past this fear and on not letting it hold them back.

Even if leaders don't experience this fear to the point of it holding them back, some of the key points below help with delivering even more effective messages.

Take Action:

To more effectively communicate to groups, do the following:

1. **Speak from the heart.**

   People most often connect with a speaker *more* if their delivery is not perfect. If we hear someone give a speech that sounds too rehearsed or delivered without feeling, we don't connect as much as we do with somebody speaking from the heart about something they care about.

Biologist and author Jane Goodall attributes her success to *"speaking to people's hearts… only when our clever brains and our human hearts work together in harmony can we achieve our true potential."*

We are moved by a speaker's message because they care about their message, even if they stumble a bit with their message. Someone else may deliver a perfectly articulated talk and not influence us at all because they showed no enthusiasm about what they were saying. They did not touch our head or our heart.

2. Focus on a few key points.

Another way to be more effective delivering a meaningful message to a group is to write down a few key points before delivering a speech or attending a meeting. This way, the message doesn't sound scripted and we can quickly get back on track if we are stuck.

Hooks or *anchors* help navigate delivering an important message to a group without sounding scripted. Decide on four or five key points (more for longer talks) and associate symbols to them that act as anchors. If we can memorize these symbols, they can anchor us to each part of our message. We can now speak naturally about our

215

topic associated with each symbol. This works well for speeches in front of large audiences and is wonderful for getting key points across in group meetings.

3. **Read about others who have overcome this fear.**

There have been many, many people who have documented their experiences overcoming the fear of speaking in front of groups. Reading about their journeys can help people with this fear see how common it really is. The stories of some of the most influential people throughout history famously experiencing and overcoming this fear include Aristotle, Isaac Newton, Mahatma Gandhi, and Abraham Lincoln.

In his autobiography, *The Story of my Experiments with Truth,* Gandhi writes a great deal about his struggles with public speaking. Examples of this from his book include, *"The presence of half a dozen people or more would strike me dumb,"* and, *"I stood up (to speak), but could not. My vision became blurred and I trembled."*

Gandhi overcame his paralyzing fear and actually saw it as his greatest advantage. He reflected later in life, *"My hesitancy in speech, which was once an annoyance, is now a pleasure. Its greatest benefit has been that it has taught me the value in economy of words... A man of few words will rarely be thoughtless in his speech; he will measure every word."*

4. Practice, practice, practice.

The experience of practicing speaking up in groups or in front of audiences again and again is one of the best ways we've found to overcome this fear. Finding out you're not going to melt or die from speaking in front of others makes it become a little easier each time. It takes intentionally doing it and putting yourself out there to get more comfortable.

Often, we coach several peers in an organization on getting their wonderful ideas and contributions into group conversations. When we are together in a group, they don't know that the person on either side of them is working on this same fear. If people knew that almost everyone experiences the same butterflies and nervousness and so many have overcome this fear, it might not seem so impossible to overcome it themselves.

Speaking more effectively in front of others can help leaders strengthen their voice and expand their *influence.* Using the energy created by a bit (or a lot) of nervousness can help enable leaders to speak enthusiastically about something they believe in.

We feel nervous because we care. Therefore, the more we can focus our energy and attention on what it is we care enough to speak about, and *not on ourselves*, the better. Ask, *"Why is my message important for others to hear?"*

The voices of *Courageous Leaders* who live and give up-close-and-personal leadership are open, eager learners who inspire others to live their best and most productive lives. *Courageous Leaders ignite* the very best potential in those they lead.

Never-ending success is accomplished by facing down our fears and self-doubts to embody *Peak to Peak Performance* in our personal and professional life. We *ignite* our *courageous self* and our *indomitable spirit* and the same in those we lead.

Personal autonomy has now transformed to our liberated voice and freedom to make and leave our world a better place.

Bibliography

1. E. S. Kim et al., *Optimism and cause-specific mortality: A prospective cohort study. Am. J. Epidemiol. 185, 21–29 (2017).*

2. Tseng, J., Poppenk, J. Brain meta-state transitions demarcate thoughts across task contexts exposing the mental noise of trait neuroticism. *Nat Commun* **11**, 3480 (2020)

3. Lehmann D, Henggeler B, Koukkou M, Michel CM *(1993) Source localization of brain electric field frequency bands during conscious, spontaneous, visual imagery and abstract thought. Brain Res Cogn Brain Res 1:203–210*

4. Lehmann D, Pascual-Marqui RD, Strik WK, Koenig T *(2010) Core networks for visual-concrete and abstract thought content: A brain electric microstate analysis. Neuroimage 49:1073–1079.*

5. Blagden J, Craske M. Effects of active and passive rumination and distraction: A pilot replication with anxious mood. Journal of Anxiety Disorders. 1996;10(4):243–252.

6. Borkovec T. The nature, functions, and origins of worry. In: Davey G, Tallis F, editors. Worrying: Perspectives on theory, assessment and treatment. Chichester: Wiley; 1994. pp. 5–33.

7. Calmes C, Roberts J. Repetitive thought and emotional distress: Rumination and worry as prospective predictors of depressive and anxious symptomatology. Cognitive Therapy and Research. 2007;30:343–356.

8. Fresco D, Frankel A, Mennin D, Turk C, Heimberg R. Distinct and overlapping features of rumination and worry: The relationship of cognitive production to negative affective states. Cognitive Therapy and Research. 2002;26(2):179–188.

9. Yu Q, Panichello MF, Cai PURPOSE, Postle BR, Buschman TJ (2020) Delay-period activity in frontal, parietal, and occipital cortex tracks noise and biases in visual working memory. PLoS Biol 18(9): e3000854.

10. Adamczyk P. D. & Bailey B. P. If not now, when? The effects of interruption at different moments within task execution. Proceedings of CHI'04 , (2004), 271-278.

11. Barnlund, Dean. "A Transactional Model of Communication." *Foundations of Communication Theory*. New York: Harper & Row, 1970.

12. 4 Factors Driving Record-High Employee Engagement in U.S., by Jim Harter, *https://purpose.gallup.com/workplace/284180/f actors-driving-record-high-employee-engagement.aspx*

13. Mehrabian, Albert (1971). *Silent Messages (1st ed.). Belmont, CA: Wadsworth.*

14. Berne, Eric. *Transactional Analysis in Psychotherapy.* Grove Press, Inc., New York, 1961.

The Lead Peak Performance Center for

Strategy, Leadership, Operational Excellence

& Personal Growth

Our *Mission*: Igniting people, teams, organizations and communities beyond current success to new levels of Peak Performance.

Our *Vision*: People in organizations and communities are strengthened to be innovative in obtaining measurable and meaningful results.

Our *Values*: Indomitable-Spirit; Humble-Urgency; Diverse-Mindedness; Other-Centered; Inspiring-Service

About the Authors

Mary L. Burkhardt, BS, MA, CAS, serves clients in their development as strategic, innovative, progressive leaders in strategy creation and engagement for execution, positioning ever-maturing leaders and team members to win in our highly competitive global marketplace and how to excel in operational excellence. Mary is recognized as a performance results leader applying innovative solutions, discipline and best practices to significantly improve sustained personal, team and company Peak to Peak Performance.

Mary helps clients make leadership and strategy everyone's job, leverage and align diversity and culture as a key performance asset, apply methods for simplifying and removing waste in business processes, consolidate functions for improved efficiency and cost reduction, and implement fast cycles of improvement and strategic transformation renewal for successful competitive advantage.

As an experienced global change agent, Mary has led people in small to worldwide organizations to be more focused on customer delight, accountable, flexible, proactive and productive as compared to the competition. She has demonstrated the ability to build performance-based cultures through proactive relationships with customers, suppliers and people across multiple organizations. Mary has held a wide range of leadership roles in public and higher education, business units, manufacturing and corporate functions including serving for a number of years as a Corporate Vice President of a Fortune 100 Company, responsible for the performance of thousands of employees.

Mary authored three books, two of which achieved #1 best-seller status.

Mary wrote the foreword to *Why Johnny Still Can't Read: A New Look at the Scandal of our Schools* by Rudolf Flesch; she was published in *Empty Pages: A Search for Writing Competence in School and Society* by Clifton Fadiman and James Howard, and she was published in *Changing Focus: What's Changing in the Business World*" by Alecia Swasy.

Mary holds a Bachelor of Science degree in Education, a Master's Degree and Post-Graduate Education in Educational Administration, and her further executive development includes the following: Finance and Accounting for Non-Financial Managers, Wharton School, University of Pennsylvania; Leadership in the 21st Century, Kenan Flagler Business School, University of North Carolina; Program for Manufacturing Excellence, Carnegie Mellon University; Statistical Thinking for Managers, Joiner Associates; Communication Skills for Managers, Ridge Associates; Lean Thinking and Simplification, Toyota; Quality Management, Dr. Edward Deming; Motorola Six Sigma; Executive Coach, Corporate Coach U and the University of Rochester.

Edward E. Davison-Gwynn, BS, certified coach, serves clients by engaging with them in leadership development, strategy development, business development and executive leadership coaching. Ed works with progressive leaders who believe in customer-pulled, employee-first cultures where enriching the lives of employees and customers is a lead indicator of success. Ed is a thought partner in helping clients reach new levels of business and personal Peak Performance.

Ed has served in numerous leadership roles in both for-profit and not-for-profit organizations. He led empowering work environments, always striving to develop team members to help them reach their highest potential. Ed led multimillion-dollar units attributing success to creating uplifting, positive cultures on teams he led where each teammate felt invested in and valued.

Ed helps lead and serves on the Board of Directors for an international not for profit that helps at-risk youth break the cycle of poverty through education.

Ed authored three books, two of which achieved #1 best-seller status.

Ed holds a Bachelor of Science Degree in International Business. Additional education and development include the following: Leadership Coaching Certification, University of Rochester; Effective Communications and Human Relations/Skills for Success Certification.

225

Further studies include: Psychology of Human Behavior; Cognitive Behavioral Therapy; Effective Communication Skills; Mysteries of Modern Physics; Einstein's Relativity and the Quantum Revolution; The Story of Human Language; The Psychology of Performance; From Yao to Mao: 5,000 years of Chinese History.

His favorite areas of interest are spending time with loved ones, reading, traveling, and spending time outdoors.

Ed's passion is leadership, specifically how inspirational leaders can transform the world.

Mary and Ed currently own and lead their company, Lead Peak Performance, LLC, where they serve a range of clients including large and small for-profits and not-for-profits, healthcare, government, education and entrepreneurs.

Services to meet their clients' needs include strategy creation and execution; leadership development that ignites and inspires; coaching for business and personal transformation; cultures of diversity, equity and inclusion; busines acumen and lean operations; and sensitive resolutions.

A Word from the Authors

Thank you for reading our book! We hope this book adds value to your life, work and those you lead.

You can sign up for our free email newsletter, *Leaders Ignite*, at our website, leadpeakperformance.com, where we deliver short, weekly Peak Performance practices to your inbox.

Please contact Mary and Ed for any questions or comments.

Mary – 1 (585) 362-9196

mary@leadpeakperformance.com

Ed – 1 (585) 414-2002

ed@leadpeakperformance.com

Please visit our website for more information:

http://LeadPeakPerformance.com

Made in the USA
Coppell, TX
14 November 2020